STALKED BY A
MOUNTAIN LION

STALKED BY A
MOUNTAIN LION

Fear, Fact, and the Uncertain Future of Cougars in America

Jo Deurbrouck

FALCONGUIDE®

GUILFORD, CONNECTICUT
HELENA, MONTANA
AN IMPRINT OF THE GLOBE PEQUOT PRESS

Falcon and FalconGuide are registered trademarks of Morris Book Publishing, LLC.

Text design: Lisa Reneson

Library of Congress Cataloging-in-Publication Data
Deurbrouck, Jo.
   Stalked by a mountain lion : fear, fact, and the uncertain future of
cougars in America / Jo Deurbrouck. — 1st Globe Pequot ed.
      p. cm. — (A Falcon guide)
   Includes bibliographical references.
   ISBN-13: 978-0-7627-4315-5
   ISBN-10: 0-7627-4315-8
   1. Puma attacks—United States. 2. Puma—Behavior—United States.
3. Human-animal relationships—United States.   I. Title.
QL737.C23D483 2007
599.75'240973—dc22

                                             2006026213

Manufactured in the United States of America
First Globe Pequot Edition/First Printing

This book is dedicated to the people whose stories fill its pages and to those who helped bring them to life.

CONTENTS

PREFACE: RETURN OF THE COUGAR

"Mountain lions are indeed back. The question is: Can we make room for them?"
—biologist Maurice Hornocker, 1992

"Anything that makes people value an animal for what it is, rather than for our fantasy of what it is, the better it is for the animal."
—biologist Sarah Durant, 1999

On January 8, 2004, Anne Hjelle and her friend Debbie Nichols went mountain biking on a popular trail in Whiting Ranch Wilderness Park, Orange County, California. Anne saw a mountain bike off the trail. The rider was not visible. She slowed. Perhaps someone needed help.

What she didn't see was the mountain lion hidden off the trail. Debbie, thirty feet behind her, did. She saw it leap upon her friend's back and knock her to the ground.

The young woman survived despite serious injuries, thanks to quick action from her friend and two passersby.

But that's not the whole story. The owner of the bike had indeed needed help. He was Mark Jeffrey Reynolds, a thirty-five-year-old amateur mountain bike racer. It's thought that his chain derailed and he stopped to fix it. His body was discovered, half-buried and partially consumed, not far from his disabled bike. A two-year-old male mountain lion was killed near the site. Human tissue was found in its stomach.

By striking coincidence these attacks occurred almost exactly a decade after California's first fatal mountain lion attack in nearly a century. The death of jogger Barbara Schoener in 1994 had rocked the state. Prior to that time California and most of the West "knew" cougars were harmless.

Mark Reynolds's death and Anne Hjelle's struggle for life were media events, but it's unlikely that anybody living in cougar country this past decade was shocked by their dramatic stories. We have read more than a few since 1994.

Called puma, mountain lion, or simply lion, the cougar is a solitary ambush hunter that preys mostly on deer. His prey often outweighs him by half, but the cougar is well-equipped for his role. His short, powerful jaws can deliver a bone-crunching bite; his long, athletic body allows him to leap twenty feet or more; and his sharp retractable claws give him the ability to cling like a burr to an elk's back.

Mountain lions are one of wildlife conservation's great success stories. Before the arrival of European settlers, they lived across North America, but by the early 1900s they had been eliminated from the American East and Midwest. As recently as the 1970s they were rarely seen even in their last stronghold, the West. To this day, many people incorrectly believe they are endangered.

Yet biologists say they now exist in healthy numbers in nearly every conducive western ecosystem, and are beginning to recolonize the Midwest. Some think they will eventually recolonize the East.

But human numbers are also increasing, and human use of the landscape is expanding even faster, especially in America's fastest growing region, the West. Today more cougars live side by side with more humans than at any previous time in history.

Mostly the relationship is a quiet one. That's the real surprise of the cougar-human story: how well we fit together. Cougars watch us walk past on forest trails. They move about our suburbs at night. They kill the occasional dog or cat. More frequently they kill livestock. But nearly always, at the approach of a human, they fade back into the brush.

Researcher Paul Beier, who compiled a much-cited list of cougar attacks in 1991, found records of only twelve U.S. attacks between 1890 and 1980. Cougar numbers were low; human numbers not yet so high. In the 1980s Beier recorded eight more. That was still only a handful, but a handful that nearly doubled the century's total.

Researching an earlier version of this book, journalist Dean Miller and I learned that the 1990s ushered in a whole new ball game. In the nine years following Beier's study, we found records of thirty-seven people attacked or killed in the United States, including Barbara Schoener. This was three times as many as in the last hundred years. In this country and Canada together, fifty-three people were injured or killed by cougars between 1990 and 1999. Statistically those are still tiny numbers. Psychologically they are not.

Researcher E. Lee Fitzhugh continues compiling attack data. Based on his ongoing work and other sources, the rate of attack has declined slightly since the 1990s. In the United States and Canada together, seventeen people were attacked by cougars between 2000 and 2005.

If you want to learn how to behave safely and responsibly in cougar country, read Steve Torres's excellent little book, *Lion Sense*. For the best recent cougar biology, read Kenny Logan's and Linda Sweanor's seminal *Desert Puma*. If you want to know what contemporary research can teach wildlife officials who are often criticized for managing by received wisdom and not by solid data, try the dry but thorough *Cougar Management Guidelines*.

If you want to take a journey through an issue that shows us at both our human best and our human worst, come with me. I am a storyteller, not a scientist or wildlife manager, but stories can illuminate issues that otherwise appear hopelessly tangled and divisive.

The stories in this book attempt to evenly light all sides of the issue of cougar-human conflict. They are inherently dramatic and as accurate as research can make them. Some hurt to read. But I think it's important to look at the pain of the child as well as the frustration of the game warden, the respect of the tracker, and the concern of the conservationist who fears we will allow one dead mountain biker to outweigh an entire species. It's important to look through the cougar's eyes as well. His world is changing dramatically and yet he continues seeking, as he has for many thousands of years, merely to exist.

Jo Deurbrouck
Idaho Falls, Idaho
August 1, 2006

1

BARBARA SCHOENER, 1994

Fog pooled in the valleys. Low clouds pressed onto the hilltops. Cool, gray drizzle hung suspended between. Spring leaves unrolled on the scrub oaks and smooth-trunked manzanita. In another month the hills outside Sacramento would resemble baked brown loaves, but on April 23, 1994, the clay trails were still soft and red, pocked by horses' hooves and mottled with fluorescent green mosses.

It was a beautiful morning to be jogging above the American River on the Western States Trail, but the three men didn't notice. They ran, walked, shouted, and stopped to listen, each absorbed by his own fears about what he might hear over the whispering rain, what he might find around the next corner.

The previous morning a woman named Barbara Schoener had driven away from the house she shared with her husband and two children for a long trail run. When she didn't return, her husband Pete came looking here, at Auburn Lake Trails. He found only her empty car. Twenty-five hours later, dozens of searchers had failed to uncover even a trace of her. It was as if vivacious Barbara Schoener had jogged straight off the planet.

And so the three men ran and worried. Thirty-seven-year-old Russ Bravard, a tall, long-legged second grade teacher, thought his friend's wife had probably tripped and fallen, injuring herself. He called as he ran, but he also scanned the trail sides carefully. She might be too weakened by her injury and the long, chilly night to respond.

Kurt Fox knew that Barbara worked with insurance companies, finding jobs for claimants who might otherwise continue to draw unemployment benefits. Some clients, Pete had explained to him, didn't want work. Sometimes they got angry. Kurt pictured the forty-year-old brunette dead beside the trail.

Ernie Flores, a big-hearted father of five, accepted Kurt's logic, but he could not picture Pete Schoener's pretty wife dead. The stocky volunteer fireman was hunting for a bad guy to fight and a woman to save.

None of the three knew Barbara well. They weren't part of the official search team. They weren't even supposed to be here. But the mystery of Barbara's disappearance and the urgency of their friend's need had compelled them to come.

Ernie remembered being surprised when his taciturn friend had begun courting an outgoing young woman who dressed sharp and smiled often. It had seemed a mismatch, but after a five-month courtship the couple married. Ten years later, when Ernie saw her at parties his runner friends occasionally hosted, he thought the two were pretty much perfect.

Russ, Kurt, and Ernie specialized in extreme distance running. The sport, called ultra running, began in the late 1970s. Its aficionados are a tight fraternity who push their bodies far beyond marathon limits: Some races are a hundred miles long. Pete was one of theirs, and Barbara had recently finished her first ultra. She had also disappeared from a trail all three trained on. It felt like a personal affront.

So at 7:00 A.M. on the morning after Barbara vanished, the three arrived at Auburn Lake Trails, a gated subdivision adjoining a cluster of foothill paths. They were met by orange-vested volunteers who told them to leave. Search-and-rescue teams were combing the hills. Everything was under control.

The men exchanged looks. Nothing needed to be said. They loitered until their presence seemed forgotten. Then they slipped under the yellow crime-scene tape strung across the trail.

Quickly, they fell into a pattern. They ran through the cold dampness, peering off the edges of the trail, calling, "Barbara!" every few yards, then stopping to listen. All they heard were the blatting blades of the search helicopters crisscrossing the sky.

What to look for? Anything. Everything. Search-and-rescue had been combing the hills on foot and horseback most of the night, but the search-and-rescue crews were not runners. They did not know the habits of runners. And they did not know these trails like Barbara did, like these three did.

Kurt kept saying, "She knows this area. She didn't get lost. Someone has to have done this."

Ernie couldn't stop the mind movies: her struggle with the faceless attacker, her abduction. "We'll get this guy," he vowed. Despite the chill he began to sweat.

Minutes later, Russ yelled. Kurt and Ernie rushed back to peer with him down a steep slope. At first Ernie couldn't tell what they were supposed to be looking at. Undergrowth on the slope was sparse—the big oaks screened sunlight in summer. All that poked through the carpet of last year's leaves were the new, leafless shoots of poison oak. So when he finally saw the white sun visor fifty feet below the trail, it lay starkly visible. It also looked cheap, like something a person would not wade through poison oak to retrieve.

Was it trash or a clue?

The men walked slowly back along the trail looking for something to either draw them down the steep slope or allow them to move on. They found it in moments: two gashes of disturbed soil, as though someone had veered precariously off the trail. The first long gash was about two feet below the trail, the second a stride below the first. If whatever had made those marks had regained the trail later, the men could find no sign of it.

Russ walked until he again stood peering down at the visor. This was a popular trail. What were the odds the disturbed soil and visor had anything to do with the missing Barbara Schoener? Russ surprised himself by beginning to edge downhill, careful of his footing and the poison oak.

In his hand the visor looked even more insubstantial than it had from above, a thing of flat foam with a knotted surgical tube strap. Thin reddish stains smeared its white surface. Russ looked at the red clay visible where his jogging shoes had scuffed up leaves. He rubbed his thumbnail into the stains on the foam. Blood or mud? He didn't know what blood would look like on a visor.

He looked again at the mud beneath his feet and decided: Someone had lost a hat in a sudden breeze and kept going. The visor in his hands had nothing to do with a missing woman and everything to do with his spooked paranoia. The stains were mud. Of course. Searchers had examined this section of trail many times since Barbara went missing. If the visor mattered, they would have picked it up.

But still.

"It's nothing. Let's go!" Kurt shouted down.

Still.

"Wait a minute." Russ scanned the hillside before him. Looked at the red stains again. Looked up. And saw something that told him the visor did indeed matter.

It was a water bottle, the kind distance runners carry, white plastic with a soft neoprene strap that snugs the bottle into the hand. Russ had one just like it. Sudden breezes might brush a visor from someone's head, but they would not snatch such a water bottle from a runner's hand.

Heedless of the poison oak, he stepped forward and picked up the bottle. It was nearly full. He found himself suddenly believing Kurt's grim scenarios.

Russ turned to scan the hillside more carefully, heavy water bottle in one hand, weightless visor in the other. Was it his imagination or was there almost a path of disturbed leaves, visible only from this angle, leading downhill from where he stood? He would later say he felt compelled, as though by something outside himself, to follow.

Ernie and Kurt half-slid down the slope after their disappearing friend. Ernie heard Russ's next words through a rustle of leaves and snapping twigs. What he remembers hearing is, "Oh my God, oh my God, oh my God."

What Russ remembers saying is a calm "She's right here."

Hidden behind a tree three hundred feet below the trail, Barbara Schoener's bare calves and jogging shoes stuck out from one end of a shallow grave. Her dark hair was barely visible on the other end. Leaves and debris obscured the rest of her. Russ stared, still caught in the compulsion that had drawn him, trying without much success not to make it into a ghost story or the hand of God. He heard Kurt and Ernie arrive but didn't turn.

"She might still be alive," Ernie's voice came to him.

They all knew she wasn't, but Ernie bent to touch her ankle. He couldn't bring himself to remove any of the obscuring debris. Her skin felt cold, the flesh rigid.

"She's dead," he heard himself say.

"What do we do?"

"We need to tell search-and-rescue," Kurt said. "Ernie, you're an EMT, right?"

Ernie nodded.

"Then you stay here."

Ernie didn't point out the illogic of this. They needed a plan, and this was as good as any. He listened to the scrabbling sounds as Russ and Kurt struggled up to the trail, then to their soft, thumping footfalls as they sprinted back along it. He was surprised by how soon the sounds faded, and by how deep the forest stillness was that they left behind. A creek, invisible somewhere below him, created a masking hiss he hadn't noticed until now.

Alone, he found he felt best lowered into an alert crouch, elbows bent, hands half-open and ready. He tried to smooth his breathing so he could hear. Probably the killer was long gone, but what if he wasn't? Almost enraged at the thought, Ernie knew he would not allow the bastard to mess with Barbara Schoener anymore. He could almost feel his hands around the man's neck. It felt good.

Then he heard a soft rustling, like feet carefully placed in leaves. He twisted toward the noise and heard it again. "The guy's still here," he thought.

Ernie was amazed to experience a sensation he'd thought was a wives' tale: The hairs rose on his arms and neck. He crouched lower and awaited the confrontation. . . .

Which did not come. Seconds passed, then minutes. Ernie heard no further sounds, but he didn't relax. He knew what he had heard. And he felt—unalone. Watched.

Some piece of an hour later, uniformed men began arriving. Two of them escorted Ernie back to Auburn Lake Trails' water-treatment plant. The plant had been the makeshift center of operations for the search. It now became headquarters for a murder investigation. Kurt and Russ were already there, waiting to be interrogated. For the first time the three men considered how police investigating a murder might interpret what they'd done, sneaking past that yellow tape.

Hours later, with no explanation and no interrogation, the men were abruptly released.

Ernie got a phone call that afternoon.

"They think it might've been a wild animal," Kurt said.

"A wild—what kind?"

"A mountain lion."

Ernie could not believe him. He had seen a grave. He had seen a murdered woman. People put people in graves. And besides, Auburn Lake Trails was the farthest thing from wilderness. The suburb's winding streets and large, tidy yards were forty-five minutes from Sacramento. Sure, you heard about animal attacks in places like, say, Alaska. Wilderness places. But not adjacent to a cloistered, gated subdivision in one of the most populous states in the nation.

No, Ernie needed there to be a murderer. He needed to hate someone, and he couldn't hate an animal.

Yet there was this: Ernie had wondered all afternoon why they had been released so suddenly. It seemed an odd way to conduct a murder investigation.

That evening, local newscasters talked nonstop about a woman killed by a cougar. Ernie watched as many broadcasts as he could find, growing less angry at the murderer he had imagined and more angry at the news shows themselves, at what seemed to him sensationalized attempts to bolster ratings at the expense of a woman who'd had the bad luck to die in an unconventional way.

And he began to feel a creeping chill at the repeated use of the word cougar, a memory of hair rising on his arms and neck, the sound of delicate footsteps. If a mountain lion had indeed killed Barbara Schoener, had it watched the three men as they stood over her body? Had it seen Russ and Kurt depart, then calculated a new set of odds in its inscrutable brain?

Had Ernie been furious when he should have been afraid?

That night at dinner, Ernie—who hates losing control—felt himself slipping. It was confusing, not having a murderer to hate. And the confusion mixed with a sense of failure at not having been able to save Barbara. He was also beginning to understand that his friend Pete would not be allowed to grieve in private. The whole world was watching, curious and horrified.

Ernie felt an odd sensation familiar from other difficult moments: He felt a part of himself seem to rise from his body into a corner of the ceiling. From that vantage he saw his healthy, safe family clustered about the table. He watched Di and his children go still as the face of the muscular, black-haired man folded into knots of anguish. The man's shoulders heaved and his head dropped into his hands. The sobbing was raw and loud. Ernie watched as Di put one hand gently on the man's arm. Ernie's two eldest sons rose from the table, silently approached their crying father, and touched their foreheads to his.

2

A CRASH COURSE IN COUGARS

Like Ernie Flores, the first officials to stand over Barbara Schoener's body saw what they expected to see: a murdered woman, face down and partially concealed in a sloppy grave.

Homicide investigators photographed the scene and painstakingly began to remove the debris blanketing Barbara Schoener's corpse. They exposed one arm, wrenched behind her back as though she had died with it tied, and what appeared to be knife wounds.

Tousled hair initially disguised what would have been the first clue that the woman had not been murdered: Most of her face was gone. The first serious doubts were raised when a massive wound was revealed beside the left shoulder blade through which most of her organs had been removed, giving her torso a deflated look.

Within a few hours it had become obvious that there was no murder to investigate. Barbara Schoener's life had been taken by something with long, conical teeth and jaws powerful enough to drive those teeth into a woman's skull. Something that inflicted wounds that resembled knife slashes. That scraped debris onto its kill, leaving a six-foot-wide swath of cleared dirt around the mound. That left behind tawny hairs. That ate flesh.

In California's history there were only two other documented fatal mountain lion attacks. Both occurred in 1909, when a woman and child died of rabies after being bitten. In recent years reports of nonfatal attacks were accumulating, but they were still such rare occurrences that most people "knew" mountain lions posed no threat to humans.

But Californians were about to get a crash course in cougars. California voters had only recently accorded the species a set of special protections. Now a cougar had done what pundits had assured those voters it would never do.

The mountain lion's scientific name, *Puma concolor*, means cat of one color, and it's nearly true. Tawny gold, gray, or tan fur fades to cream on his belly. Cream and dark brown patch his face. Darker fur may stripe his spine or tip his tail and ears.

A solitary hunter, the mountain lion is one of North America's few large native carnivores and arguably its most proficient. While they mostly prey on deer, adult lions have been known to take bull elk weighing six hundred pounds and armed with sharp hooves and a rack of branched antlers that can weigh forty pounds.

Like most cats, the mountain lion's curved claws are retractable, which protects the claws and keeps them sharp. When the animal flexes them, they arc together like tandem fishhooks. A large lion, weighing 150 pounds and measuring eight feet from nose to tail tip, may have claws an inch long. Lions in excess of 200 pounds have been documented.

The lion's teeth say their owner is strictly a carnivore. The four long canines are conical, made to hold prey and separate skeletal joints when feeding. The small front incisors are spaced close to remove hair and feathers and strip flesh from bone. Cougar premolars and molars have no flat chewing surfaces. Instead they are sharply ridged, enabling the animal to shear dense muscle tissue. Bulging cheek muscles and short, blocky jaws deliver a bone-crunching bite. Unlike humans, cougars cannot shift their lower jaw from side to side, cannot chew. What they gain by this is a bite as precise as a trap.

Unlike wolves, which typically run larger prey to exhaustion before attempting a kill, the lion tires quickly. A big male can reach speeds of forty miles per hour in less than fifty feet, can leap fifteen feet vertically and forty horizontally, but he cannot maintain that level of exertion. So he adds to his formidable strength and speed a characteristic hunting style: ambush.

Surprise adds a safety factor for an animal that cannot afford injury.

The morning after Barbara's body was found, professional trackers with specially trained hounds arrived at Auburn Lake Trails. It was the hunters' job to fill in as many details that rain and the tramping feet of searchers had left intact, and then to locate and kill the lion. The public would almost certainly demand it. It also seemed reasonable to assume that the cat which had chosen human prey once might do so again. Most of all, officials wanted to examine the cougar's body and answer the question everyone was asking, "What was wrong with this animal that it had done what cougars do not do?"

The houndsmen were told it was imperative to find out.

Based on the trackers' findings and the story written on Barbara Schoener's body, this is what probably happened the last morning of the runner's life and what later happened to the mountain lion with whom she crossed paths.

———————

Barbara drove through the manned gate of Auburn Lake Trails subdivision, giving the guard the name of a friend who lived there, then dropping the visitor pass on her dashboard. She could get to the trailhead without entering the gated community, but it took longer and Barbara liked to be efficient. She drove past big, daffodil-sprinkled yards. They were empty this early in the morning but soon would fill with playing children and adults washing cars and mowing lawns. Then she was past the houses and into dense oak forest.

Moments later she parked her Dodge Intrepid at Gate #3 and began her warm-up routine. She wore purple shorts, white Nikes, and a hooded purple sweatshirt. When she finished, she slipped her car key into her shorts pocket and pulled a Fleet Feet visor—white foam with a surgical tubing strap—over her short brown hair. She slid thin white gloves up over her perfectly lacquered nails, grabbed her water bottle, and began to jog. It was 8:00 A.M.

As she warmed, Barbara stripped off the sweatshirt and knotted it about her waist. The morning air poured like cool water across her bare arms. Less than an hour into her run she began to jog around a long, U-shaped curve that, at its apex, overlooked the American River far below and the rumpled hills stepping up its far side. The distant river whispered in her ears.

Barbara was new to ultra running and enjoying it. She had entered her first race only a month before. Perhaps as she rounded that corner she was remembering the day of the Cool Canyon Run, how strong she'd felt at the end, surprising herself, and how she'd urged her lagging, long-legged husband, "C'mon, Mr. P. Let's finish together."

But Pete Schoener was nearly spent. "No, you go on. Don't wait for me," he gasped.

She'd surprised herself again by being able to pull reluctantly ahead.

Or perhaps she was simply concentrating on her stride and foot placement. She would have been wary of twisting an ankle so far from her car. The previous night, after their son's Little League game, she and Pete had discussed this day's logistics. Since Andrew had another game, they couldn't both run. Pete volunteered to take the boy. Protective of his wife, he suggested Barbara use a trail frequented mostly by horseback riders and other runners, where she was unlikely to be harassed. The route he suggested would take her seventeen miles to Brown's Ridge and back on the Western States Trail. Although Barbara knew the trail well, this was only her fourth long practice run alone.

Somewhere in the first miles of that Saturday's run, Barbara Schoener, five feet eight and 140 pounds, attracted the attention of another athlete. The female lion was two or three years old, the equivalent of a human teenager or young twenty-something, and weighed eighty-two pounds. She stood less than two feet at the shoulder, shorter than a big golden retriever. But cougars are long-bodied: On hind legs she could have stared Barbara in the eyes.

She looked nothing like the mountain lions in calendar shots. Nearly all commercial mountain lion photos are of cage-reared cats who can afford their telltale, sagging paunches. Wild lions, like this female, are lean and strapped with muscle, from their Popeye-like forelegs to their knotted haunches.

She had large greenish eyes and a long tail held in a low J curve.

She shadowed the loping human from above, keeping pace in the characteristic posture of the cougar, head thrust forward below high, rolling shoulder blades. Her long, powerful hind legs propelled her across the hillside. She moved with such grace that her big paws seemed to barely brush the ground.

She was a thing of beauty. And up until this moment, she had also been, against the odds, a success.

At one time cougars occupied nearly all of both North and South America. Although the life of the solitary carnivore is precarious—meals come pre-equipped with teeth, spines, sharp hooves, or antlers, and every neighboring mountain lion is a potentially lethal competitor—cougars are wonderfully adapted to it. But increasing human population and accelerating habitat changes have created a number of new risks. This young cougar had had to learn about automobiles, for instance. In some lion populations cars are the primary cause of death. And she'd had to avoid learning that livestock were easy and safe to kill, full of good fat and high nutrition. If she had killed livestock, even in California, she would likely have been taken by a hunter with a depredation permit.

In any cougar state but California she would also have had to survive annual sport hunting quotas that can reach 20 percent or more of the adult population. One hunted population of cougars studied in Wyoming had, as its oldest adult, a seven-year-old (cougars in captivity live twenty years or more). Another researcher had to move his study site after nearly all of his first winter's fourteen collared cougars were shot before spring snowmelt. The states in which cougar populations are highest also have the fastest growing human populations. Nowhere is this more true than California. This cougar had had to learn to hunt and mate, travel and sleep, raise young and survive, all without drawing undue human attention.

Given all these new risks piled atop already harsh odds, it's somewhat astounding that, in the mid-1990s, cougars were no longer at all rare in Barbara Schoener's backyard, the Sierra foothills. This fact would have surprised her and many other residents, particularly since the animals were so rarely sighted.

One reason for the lions' near invisibility is their low population density. A forest "full" of lions holds only a handful of adults. A region that supports one thousand black bears might contain an adult population of one hundred lions.

Mountain lions are primarily crepuscular, sleeping in brushy daybeds or resting near kills during the day and hunting at dawn and dusk. One study indicated that 90 percent of a cougar's movements occur in darkness, during the hours humans tend to be indoors.

Few animals move with such studied, slow grace or, when called upon, such speed. Few hunt with more silent efficiency.

The upshot? A cougar that does not want to be observed probably won't be.

So although cougars live in almost every western forest, desert, or canyon land that contains both deer and cover from which to hunt (this includes more than 60 percent of California), few humans have reason to know it. Even cougar researchers seldom see the animals they study unless they've trapped or treed one. Skilled hunters can find sign in cougar country without great difficulty, but if they want to see the actual animal they have to release their hounds on the track so the dogs can bark the cougar up a tree.

Barbara Schoener may have been followed that day for several miles, the cat loping smoothly through the heavy manzanita and scrub oak above the trail. As the woman jogged around the American River overlook, the cougar cut across the U-shaped bend. Where the trail straightened north into brushy shadow, she waited for the human to reappear. Her prints would later tell the trackers all this. But what was not to be read in the sign was, What motivated her?

Perhaps at this point it was simple feline curiosity. She had probably watched or followed people before, enthralled as she was by most anything that moved, whether her belly was full or empty.

Where the trail straightened north, it reentered heavier brush. The river's whisper was still in Barbara's ears but fainter than her own breathing. The steep bank on her left was about six feet high. The hillside dropped precipitously on her right. Lions frequently hunt steep slopes, tackling their prey from above, letting gravity add force to that all-important first impact. In addition, the dense brush may have screened the trail from the cat's view. If so, she heard Barbara's running approach before she saw her.

Experience had taught her that a running creature was not an attentive one. Then the woman burst into sight, already past and apparently running away.

Maybe it was that simple, but it's hard not to want an additional catalyst for the moment that followed, a reason that this lion attacked this woman at this place and time. Nearly every cougar alive has probably passed up more than one such opportunity. If there was such a trigger—Barbara suddenly increasing her pace, or making a sound of discomfort as she landed awkwardly on a stone, or perhaps something about the way she smelled—we'll never know.

What we do know is that Barbara was unaware, the lion's belly was not full, and she hunted for two. She was a first-time mother and her seven-week-old kitten was hidden nearby.

The cat's silent leap was well-timed. Lost in her runner's reverie, Barbara's first warning was the sensation of being violently pushed downhill. She felt sharp stabs in her shoulders and neck and a sudden, staggering weight upon her back. She reflexively struggled to stay upright on the steep slope but managed only a few stumbling steps before she fell. The cat rode her sliding body for forty-five feet until they were both brought to a stop by a fallen fir.

Mountain lions often miss that first critical leap, but the cat that succeeds can probably expect to kill with merciful efficiency. Longtime Montana houndsman Bob Wiesner puts it this way: "If a lion knocks them down, the prey doesn't get away."

But Barbara Schoener was not a deer. She had arms that could reach behind her head, hands that could grab. She lacked the long, curved ungulate neck whose vulnerabilities the lion intimately understood. The typical lion-killed deer has a few deep wounds about the head and neck and almost no other damage until the cougar begins to feed. But human victims like Barbara Schoener may be bitten dozens of times about the face, neck, torso, and especially the arms and hands, apparently in an effort by the cat to subdue the victim after the initial attack inexplicably fails to incapacitate. These bites can be severe: Some of the gashes in Barbara's hands exposed bone. A fingertip was found inside a bloody glove near her body.

However long it lasted, the battle probably occurred in silence.

Contrary to the Hollywood image of the snarling, spitting mountain lion, the big cats' victims almost always report a silent attack.

The story told by Barbara's wounds is important. Since her death, other adults have fought lions, sometimes barehanded, and lived. Some have not. Did Barbara have a chance to save herself? And if so, how? Or was she already all but dead when a hungry lion, willing to try something new, noticed her jogging along the Western States Trail?

I have been offered several versions of the moments following the cat's initial leap. Two are worth describing here.

The official one, published in area newspapers after the attack and based on forensics and other evidence found at the site, is that after the slide downhill, Barbara regained her feet. Where Russ Bravard would later stand holding her visor, she faced her attacker and fought back. It was at this time that she received the bites on both arms and hands. She left her blood in the freshly broken branches of the fallen fir at her back. Then she turned and fled downhill, a fatal error. The bite that cracked her skull and ended her life was delivered from behind as she fell again twenty-five feet further down the slope.

The second version belongs to a professional tracker and lion hunter who says he has examined at least two thousand cougar-killed deer and other animals. Reading the clues remaining on the slope two days after Barbara died, Dave Fjelline believes she never regained her feet after that first, disorienting slide, never even saw the animal that killed her. The cat was straddling the woman as they came up against the downed tree. It held her to the slick clay. One arm pinned beneath her body, Barbara reached back with the other, trying to grab whatever clung there, or perhaps simply trying to protect her damaged neck.

Fjelline believes that the lion bit deeply into Barbara's neck, ripping an artery. Arterial bleeding is fast and violent. Blood sprayed into the fir's branches. Blood loss began to subdue the woman even before the bite that fractured her skull. As cougars do, the animal then dragged her further from the trail so that she and her kitten could feed in peace.

If the official version is correct, by fleeing in panic Barbara Schoener forfeited her life. Cougars seem to find flight utterly compelling. That probably goes double if the fleeing creature is injured.

Those who survive cougar attacks are, almost universally, those who stand their ground or whose companions stand for them. But if Fjelline is right, Barbara never had a solid chance to defend herself.

After her meal the female did what lions everywhere do: She raked debris over her kill. Approximately seventy-five searchers, some with dogs, combed the area from midafternoon Saturday until midnight. They traveled on horseback, foot, and mountain bike. They carried powerful flashlights that they trained here and there. They saw nothing.

Later that night as the forest quieted, the cougar uncovered her kill and moved it another thirty-five feet from the trail. The forest was full of human presence, but cougars often do this anyway, sometimes moving a kill several times in search of a good hiding spot and, perhaps, cool, meat-preserving shade.

During the night she brought her kitten to the spot. The hash of tiny punctures found on the dead woman's side probably mark the antics of a playful infant. The mother cougar was protective of her only kitten. Likely he'd had littermates that had not survived even this far: The typical litter size is three. A human observer would have found him adorable. He looked like an oversized, speckled infant house cat. If he lived long enough to lose those spots and the porcelain blue eyes of infancy, he would be lucky indeed. The odds can be as low as one in four against a cougar kitten reaching adulthood.

Protected by darkness, the mother fed again. Perhaps the infant did too: He was being weaned. Then the cat again hid her kill.

When the sky lightened, the mother cougar padded to the creek for water. Then she picked a hidden place to digest her meal, play with her kitten, groom her short, dense fur with a sandpaper tongue, and wait out the day. Cougars have several competitors besides man. Bears, coyotes, and wolves can all usurp cougar kills. Wolves and grizzlies were long gone from California, but black bears were common and, across much of the country, the elimination of the wolf has been an invitation for the resilient coyote to thrive. So the cougar wanted be near her kill, although not too near.

But the unwanted attention this young cougar had already drawn to herself and her tiny, spotted kitten had to be more than her feline brain could imagine.

The next night, as Ernie Flores sobbed in the arms of his family, the drizzle that had grayed the sky all day turned to rain. Water pooled in the slight depression from which Barbara's body had been pulled by investigators.

The mother cougar was hungry and her kill had disappeared, several nights of life-giving meat carried off as she watched from the undergrowth. And although cougar mothers often stash multiple kills in an area, this female had no others. She needed to hunt.

Her kitten was far too young to keep up. She nudged him into dense brush or into a defensible slot between two boulders. Cougar mothers and kittens speak to one another in birdlike, chirruping sounds. They also purr. Perhaps she settled her kitten in this way before she left him.

The kitten's job was to avoid attracting predators in the darkness. The mother's job was to kill, feed herself so she remained strong, and then return for her kitten or bring him to the meat.

That same night, telephone calls crisscrossed the region as houndsmen organized to search for a killer cat. In the days that followed, hairs found at the site were examined: They belonged to a cougar. An autopsy was performed on Barbara Schoener. The clearest bite was photographed, measured, and compared to bite patterns from lion skulls. Lion teeth must work perfectly, so the dental variation found among humans doesn't exist in cougars. It has been hypothesized that a cougar unlucky enough to break a single canine may soon starve. Even the rate of tooth wear in aging lions is predictable. Forensics experts decided, based on their sample bite and on tracks found at the scene, that they were looking for either an immature male cougar or a mature female.

During the following nights, the cougar crisscrossed her territory, conducting her own hunt. Trackers later found no indication that she killed any large prey in those days. Perhaps luck was not with her. The cougar is a consummate hunter but deer, hunted by cougars probably as long as the two species have existed, are equally wary. She may have settled for raccoons or other small prey or she may have gone hungry.

Meanwhile, the cougar was being written about in newspapers across the nation. She became the primary preoccupation of local California Fish and Game officials and the cause of a storm of paperwork.

Five trackers and their hounds, dogs capable of detecting a lion's scent in the air thirty minutes after it has passed or of catching the smell in a cat's tracks days later, mapped the area and began, methodically, to hunt. A team of scientists was on hot standby, ready to conduct a necropsy, an autopsy of the animal in the event the hunters succeeded. The scientists' goals would be, first, to make sure the houndsmen had killed the right cat and, almost as important, to find an explanation for what nearly everyone agreed was horribly aberrant behavior.

In addition to telephones, radios, vehicles, guns, and well-trained hounds, the human hunters had in their favor a knowledge of lions. Despite the vast, folded terrain reaching high into the Sierras and down into cultivated farmland, this was no needle-in-a-haystack search. Dave Fjelline and his fellow hunters knew, for instance, that cougars almost always stay near their kills and often revisit old kill sites. And since adult lions are territorial, any adult found in the area could be viewed with suspicion. Although Dave and his hunters didn't know about the kitten, its existence played in their favor as well: The territories of lion mothers collapse when their kittens are young.

Knowledge of cats also allowed the houndsmen to feel assured of their own safety, despite the fact that they hunted an animal that had just killed a human. Conducted intelligently, a cougar hunt is simply not dangerous work. This is because cougars tend to behave in ways that, in a human, would be called timid. It's a rare mountain lion, for instance, that won't leap into a tree when it hears dogs howling on its trail. Many hunters choose to use only one or two dogs, each half the size of its prey. An adult cougar could make short work of these dogs if it chose to, but they almost never do.

The hunters blocked out an area about a mile square with the site of Barbara's death as its approximate center. The American River delineated one side, a subdivision another, and trails the other two sides. They began at the perimeter, examining and measuring every cougar track that entered or left. They found no match. Then they started working their way in.

Days passed. Dave Fjelline knew that the odds of finding the right animal were fading, particularly if the killer was a subadult male. Males who have not established adult territories can wander huge distances. And if the hunters did kill a likely cougar, the opportunity to prove that it was the right animal was fading faster still. The cougar's digestive tract would have quickly eliminated the most obvious evidence. Other evidence, like human blood and skin snagged under its claws, might remain for only a few days longer. Dave wished officials had had the sense to replace the body they took away with a fresh deer kill, perhaps enticing the cougar to stay in the area. He would have bet anything that when the body was removed, the cougar was near, perhaps very near indeed.

On Sunday, May 1, eight days after Barbara Schoener died, Dave Fjelline crossed the first fresh cougar tracks the hunters had seen in days. They were medium-sized, those of an adult female or subadult male. They pointed toward the kill site a quarter mile away. Dave had a feeling the houndsmen's luck had turned.

Cliff Wylie and his dogs, searching along the Western States Trail, crossed cougar tracks a few minutes later. He followed them to the point where Barbara Schoener had been knocked from the trail. The hounds began hauling excitedly at their leashes. They smelled a cougar and not just on the ground. They were air scenting.

Nobody knows why cougars return to old kill sites, but they frequently do. In fact lions have been known to revisit kills so old that only scraps of bone and hair remain. There they renew "scratches" or scent markers, or pick up a bone to play with. Perhaps they sniff out which scavengers have been drawn to the spot and how recently.

Cliff knew that the lion whose track he followed was almost certainly Barbara Schoener's killer. He unsnapped his dogs' leashes. The hounds bounded down the slope.

Minutes later Cliff stood at the base of a black oak staring at a female lion twenty feet over his head. He was three-hundred yards from where Barbara's body had been found. Dave Fjelline and houndsman John Nicholas had released their dogs on the track as well. An unruly pack now barked and leaped at the base of the tree.

Treed lions often seem to feel secure, lolling across a branch and blinking sleepily at the frantic hounds below. But this cat looked tense. Her tail tip twitched nervously. Her eyes darted. Cats that looked that way sometimes leaped. Should Cliff shoot her before she did? It wasn't impossible that she was the wrong cat, and all of California was following the final scenes of this drama. There had already been public outcry at the fact that hunters were seeking to kill a lion.

He called Dave on his radio. She's treed but nervous, he said. What should he do?

"Hey, you know what needs to be done," Dave replied, and began hurrying toward the tree. Thirty seconds later, a single shot cracked through the oak forest. For fear of repercussions, the name of the hunter who fired that shot was not released.

The necropsy confirmed it: This cat had killed Barbara Schoener. Material scraped from under the claws of the lion's right front paw was DNA tested and found to be human. Barbara Schoener, along with about 11 percent of the population, had this particular type of DNA.

Exhaustive tests were run in hopes of finding that the animal had suffered from a disease, rabies maybe. But there would be no comforting answer: She appeared normal and healthy. She was lactating, however. Which meant that somewhere near the spot where first Barbara and then the lion had died, one or more kittens was likely starving.

The Department of Fish and Game was inundated by concerned and even angry calls. They had killed a mother, orphaned helpless babies. "Barbara Schoener was a mother too," replied one astounded official.

A second search began. Three days later a single dehydrated, weakened kitten was found among a jumble of granite just above the Western States Trail, probably at the exact spot where his mother had hidden him on the morning she was killed.

The kitten was given a name: Willow. His new home was the Folsom Zoo, where Pete Schoener, craggy and solemn-faced even in levity, occasionally visited with his and Barbara's children.

The family also sometimes visited the commemorative resting bench that Pete and other runners had built on the panoramic bend close to where Barbara had died. In his early teens Andrew Schoener liked to collect salamanders from the nearby creek, and beetles and other bugs from the carefully laid rock stairs below the memorial. He took them home in glass jars.

Pete liked to sit on the bench. He tried to picture how Barbara had looked as she breezed out the door that last time. He had been careful not to ask officials too many questions about what happened a few hours later. He didn't want to learn anything that might steal from him the hope that Barbara hadn't suffered.

From the stone bench Pete could stare out at the hills and down at the river. It's a peaceful place. Frequent breezes stir the leaves of the oaks, and a whispery cool water sound wells and fades in the distance. Despite what happened to his wife here, Pete knew that this was not a dangerous place, as places go. He enjoyed the view. He remembered his wife. He kept a watchful eye on their children.

3
JIM MEPHAM, 1992

By the time Barbara Schoener died in 1994, cougar sightings were on a dramatic upswing. Cougar attacks, while rare, were clearly increasing as well. Since 1980 not a year had passed without at least one. This worried cougar advocates. They believed that despite its spectacular comeback, without human tolerance the cougar was finished. And how tolerant would people be of an animal, no matter how mysterious and gloriously wild, that lived in the woods behind your house—and occasionally ate people?

The fact that some cougar country residents would find the rise in conflicts alarming, out of proportion to the statistical risk was at first misjudged by game agencies and policymakers. The official line remained that cougars were harmless, or close enough. So when conflicts occurred, some people felt lied to. "I didn't even know there were cougars in these woods," one Spokane-area woman complained after her dog was mauled. She wasn't sure whose job it had been to tell her, but she had no doubt it was somebody's.

Cougar populations had rebounded enough to teach us what coexistence with a large obligate carnivore looked like. Our next job was to learn how to stare this new coexistence squarely in the face. Only a few years later, game agencies increasingly did just that: They no longer attached the word "harmless" to the mountain lion. Sightings were taken much more seriously, but with a response more often directed toward educating humans than neutralizing cats because the dawning realization that cougars *will* kill people can obscure a more basic fact of cougar-human coexistence: Cougars kill to eat, and humans are far from their favorite meal.

Few cougar stories illustrate this as well as Jim Mepham's. The Montana wildlife photographer put himself in harm's way one spring day only to find that harm was uninterested in him.

A high school science teacher as well as a photographer, Jim Mepham lived with his young wife in East Glacier, a tiny Montana town tucked into the shoulder of Glacier National Park. The park is home to black bears, grizzlies, and Jim's favorite subjects, mountain goats.

In 1992 spring came early. The promise of new green against cobalt sky made Jim want to visit his favorite goat spot, Walton Goat Lick in Glacier National Park. He dressed in a long-sleeved white T-shirt and light-colored khaki pants. He wanted to get close to mountain goats, and mimicking the coloring of one couldn't hurt. On his way out the door, he grabbed a few handfuls of film from the refrigerator and an expensive new lens he'd convinced his wife he needed, despite the hole it punched in their budget. The rest of his camera gear lived in a padded backpack in his truck.

By 11:00 A.M. he and fellow photographer Steve Torno stood a mile above the goat lick on a steep shale slope. A herd of perhaps thirty goats grazed above them. The animals' thick winter coats shone cloud-white against the sky.

Mepham loved the goats' narrow profiles, their long, bearded faces, their almond eyes, the lips curving into what would, on human faces, be gentle grins. He loved the way they danced on precise, tippy-toed hooves over ground that made him grab for handholds. And although this day's work was just off the highway, he loved the high, rocky crags that goats typically frequented. Goats have a pretty good view of the world, he liked to tell people. With his new lens, he knew he was getting crisp images. *Montana Magazine* was looking for a goat picture for its cover and maybe one of these would work.

Since this was in Glacier National Park, Walton Goat Lick was also grizzly bear habitat. Anyone in his right mind is cautious around the short-tempered grizzly, so the two men had a preexisting bear plan: If confronted, they would stand together and face the animal. Jim usually carried pepper spray, an aerosol bear deterrent. If necessary, he would use it to protect them both.

But Jim figured the grizzlies were still hibernating. And as he'd parked the truck an hour before, he'd seen goats just above the road. He was impatient to be shooting. So he hurriedly slipped an extra lens and a dozen rolls of film into his pockets, attached the beautiful new lens to a camera body, affixed both to the head of his tripod, and strode up Snowslide Gulch. Left behind was his camera pack. In a holster on its hip-belt was the pepper spray.

Snowslide Gulch falls steeply from high country down to the Middle Fork of the Flathead River. At river's edge the gray cliffs of Walton Goat Lick bleed sodium, potassium, calcium, and magnesium. In order to replenish these minerals in their winter-worn bodies, the goats come down every spring and summer to lick at the ground. They come in such numbers that Highway 2 has been fenced off with chain link, directing the animals into a specially built Snowslide Gulch goat underpass. Fence and underpass together concentrate goat traffic in the ravine until their trails lace the steep hillside. Wispy flags of white hair festoon the twiggy knapweed. To a goat photographer—or a carnivore—those trails and that hair present a nearly irresistible invitation.

Jim was comfortable shooting here. He visited Snowslide Gulch so often that his feet had memorized the loose shale-littered slope. Over his shoulder he could see his red Nissan parked beside the highway less than a half mile away. And since he didn't have to be alert for grizzlies, for an hour he lost himself entirely to his clicking shutter and the slow grazing approach of the goats in his viewfinder.

When the herd spooked, Jim's first reaction was bemusement: How odd, he thought, that he and Steve had sparked a panicked flight that streamed downhill *toward* them. Luckily, the men had positioned themselves at the base of a rock outcrop, its top several feet above their heads. Before the stampede, they'd been photographing goats posed against the sky on that outcrop. Within moments, goats were leaping from and streaming around it, barely missing the two men. Jim and Steve shrunk reflexively against the rock, but Jim's camera remained pointed at the goats.

What Jim saw next was a nanny running shoulder to shoulder with the herd, made desperately alone by what rode her: A big tawny animal draped across her back like a muscular rug, head twisted to bury its teeth in her throat. To Jim the mountain lion seemed bigger and more vital than the goat to which it clung.

By reflex, Jim tracked with his lens. But during the next ten seconds, his index finger did not once compress the shutter button, even though goat and lion passed so close that their images blurred. This was the fourth wild lion Jim had seen, and the first near enough to photograph. This was the most dramatic event that had ever unfolded in front of his camera. But he wasn't ready.

Fifty feet below, the cat rode the crumpling goat to the ground, then lay across her with his teeth still buried in her throat. Silently the cougar waited. Just as silently, her sweet, patient smile still in place, the goat died. Her comrades ran downslope for another 200 yards before slowing.

Although they might have assumed themselves in danger—they were interlopers and fresh meat lay before them on the ground—Jim and Steve didn't consider leaving. Jim knew the solitary mountain lion was seldom photographed in the wild. Most commercial wildlife images and nearly all marketable cougar photos are taken on game farms, where fences and feeding stations make for cooperative subjects. Jim's insistence on selling only images of free-ranging animals had placed him in company with a disadvantaged elite who rely on luck as much as hard work and talent for their shots. Given this incredible opportunity—and the possibility that he might capture at least the end of the story on film—he wasn't going anywhere.

Besides, Jim probably felt he *was* armed. True, he didn't have his bear spray or a gun, but he carried an invisible shield: the confidence of the species that invented those weapons.

Autowinders quietly whirring, he and Steve exposed frame after frame. Minutes passed before the lion released its hold on the limp white neck. Then it raised its head to stare up the steep slope, its lips curling deliberately back to reveal long, curved canines. Jim recognized with a shock that the threat was directed at him and Steve. The cat's eyes seemed to seek his through the viewfinder. But then, as if its point had been made, the big animal rose and faded into some low brush, the warning unmistakable. Proof of the cougar's lethal skill lay below them. Besides, they were clearly forcing the cat from its meal. The men began picking their way back toward the truck.

Below them, the herd had gone back to browsing. Jim began again to enjoy the windless, warm air. Sunlight drew sparkling color from new green shoots, ruddy rock, white goats. Jim was already rethinking their decision to leave. There was no sign of the lion. It was probably circling back to its kill now that the men had moved away. Hesitantly at first, but then with greater absorption, Jim and Steve began again to frame and snap goat images. One would later become the magazine cover Jim had hoped for.

The goats browsed up Snowslide Gulch, away from the dead nanny and toward a small, intersecting ravine. As they moved out of shooting range, Jim noticed a new nanny band, about five females and yearlings, coming into sight a half mile away, picking their way down Snowslide Gulch. The new nannies would also cross the little ravine. Jim and Steve began to work toward them.

Jim tried not to think about how he had missed the priceless gift of those first images. Everything had happened so fast, the details were already fading. Even the memory of the cougar's silent warning couldn't stop him from wishing he could relive those moments.

Soon the men found themselves on an outcrop—brick-red stone dulled by gray lichens—overlooking the small ravine. The new nanny band was approaching its far side; they were almost in photo range. The men waited.

Then Jim saw the lion. It crouched at the edge of some alders. Like the men, it watched the little band. If Jim hadn't known a lion was near, he'd never have seen it, even when it began to move. Its low-bellied stalk was so painstaking that the next five minutes brought it only twenty feet closer to the goats. It advanced by gliding a few feet forward, freezing into a cat-shaped rock, then gliding forward again.

The men knew they should go—they were way too close, barely a hundred feet away. Instead they balanced their tripods on the outcrop. Jim's heart pounded, and his hands shook so hard that without the tripod he couldn't have worked. The shaking came from excitement though, not fear. He was sure he was about to be given a second chance at his once-in-a-lifetime shots. He could not believe his luck.

The goats grazed slowly toward the draw. The lion inched slowly toward the goats. If either were aware of the humans, neither gave any indication.

Finally, lion and goats were only fifteen feet apart. Jim thought he could see the cat tremble with tension. If the goats looked up, the lion would be in plain sight. The sure-footed animals could scatter and flee. But they didn't look up.

The lion uncoiled. In one long bound it landed on a nanny, burying its face in her thick mane. The nanny careened straight toward the two men. She struggled to keep her feet beneath her, as though she understood falling meant death, and threw her head and shoulders from side to side but didn't—or couldn't—hook her tormentor with her little black horns. *Click*, went Jim's shutter.

With no hesitation the nanny charged off the ravine's fifteen-foot wall. Goat and cat separated briefly and flew, stretched necks and front legs pointing toward the ravine's floor. *Click*. They landed side by side barely twenty feet from Jim, filling his viewfinder. The goat crumpled as she hit. The cougar fell too but rose immediately, dropping onto her and regaining that patient, throat-squeezing bite. *Click*.

The goat's white hair was unstained by her dying. Jim heard no growls, no piteous cries, only the anxious scrambling of the remaining goats, the irrelevant—and distant—sound of cars on the highway, and the whir of his camera drive. He reloaded once, wincing at the additional noise. *Click. Click. Click.*

As he shot, Jim's excitement again gave way to uncertainty. Before the lion's leap, the men had been separated from the animals by a cliff and the little ravine. Now there were only a few yards of thin air and the tall boulders upon which they stood between them and the powerful predator. If it chose, the animal could probably reach them in one athletic bound.

Maybe we should leave, Jim thought. *Click*.

Then the cat raised its head, stared at the photographers, and parted its jaws. It rose, teeth still visible, and padded slowly to the base of the rock. Fifteen feet above its silent snarl, Jim suddenly felt more terrified than he'd ever been in his life. He also realized he was alone. Without registering its significance, he'd been hearing for several moments the clattering rocks and snapping brush that marked Steve's rapid retreat.

Amazed at his foolhardiness and dispassionately noting that his knees had begun to actually bang together, Jim shot frame after frame of the cougar's upturned snarl. The pacing cat seemed to measure the distance that separated them. The message was clear: Jim was invited to leave. But he couldn't stop shooting. He'd never seen pictures like the ones he was getting, not even from game-farm photographers.

Then the lion swung away and began to loop around the left side of the outcrop. For a moment Jim was relieved. Then he knew, as clearly as if the cat had spoken its intentions, that in moments it would reappear on the hillside behind him. It would claim the advantage of higher ground. It would also stand between Jim and his red Nissan truck, which in the corner of his eye suddenly looked toy-like and very distant.

Clarity struck. This was not about photographs. It was about living or dying.

Jim grasped the heavy Boden tripod by its legs. This created a weapon four feet long. At its business end was his new two thousand dollar lens on his favorite Nikon camera body. He figured if the cat came fast, he'd get one good swing. Improbably, a tiny corner of his mind occupied itself imagining how he'd explain to his wife that he'd broken the new lens on its first trip out.

Then he fled backward, tripod extended toward the outcrop, stumbling up the steep slope.

He was twenty-five yards away when the cat looped around the outcrop and back into view. At this moment, Jim's lion encounter became exactly like the vast majority of frightening lion encounters. The animal had just demonstrated an easy and fatal prowess. Jim was stumbling awkwardly up the same unstable slope that had assisted the cougar in its first goat kill. Yet the animal did not follow.

Instead the cougar stepped onto the crumbly red outcrop and placed its big paws where Jim's feet had been moments before. Its ears, which had been lowered, rose straight from its small, round head, and its jaws were neatly closed. But its eyes did not release him. Again, the message seemed clear: Leave right now. Or else. This time, Jim accepted the invitation.

4

VANCOUVER ISLAND

When startling cougar encounters and attacks began to make news in America in the 1980s, baffled officials turned their eyes to a mountainous island off Canada's west coast.

Almost half of all recorded cougar attacks had occurred there, in a place barely bigger than Vermont. Even in the 1990s, as attacks increased sharply across the American West, little Vancouver Island still accounted for over a third of them.

Although half of the twentieth century's cougar victims still comprise a tiny number (thirty-seven to be exact), everyone on the island seems to have a great cougar story. It's as if, in this one place, the normally reclusive cougar *tries* to make headlines.

While most residents of cougar country never see their feline neighbors, Vancouver Island resident Glenn Galbraith has seen three. The first two were in the 1980s when he worked at a pulp mill in a small timber town on the northwest coast. Both times he was jogging and surprised the cats. Both ran away. In the United States at that time, either of those sightings would have made a startling tale.

But it was the third cougar that gave him a Vancouver Island story to tell. Galbraith was driving to work when the car in front of him slowed. He could see a bicyclist pedaling down the shoulder. He assumed that was the reason for the slowdown. But then a golden shape appeared in mid-air behind the cyclist, wriggling and pawing at nothing during its impressive hang-time. The cougar landed in the far lane and disappeared into the ditch. The driver ahead of Galbraith later said the animal had been chasing the bicycle's rear tire for a hundred yards before that dramatic leap. The cyclist had missed it all. The men had trouble convincing him they weren't pulling his leg.

Vancouver Island's most dramatic cougar stories aren't necessarily recent. One night in 1951, a sixty-three-year-old telephone-line worker far up the island's east coast saw a cougar pacing outside his cabin. When Eddie McLean turned off his gas lantern at about 9:00 P.M., the animal crashed through the cabin window. McLean struggled with it in the dark, groped for and found his knife, then slashed at it. When the animal broke free, McLean fled into the night in his underwear. He climbed into his boat and rowed five miles to a nearby empty cabin. He was found there the next morning, weak from blood loss and exposure. The cat was found similarly weakened on McLean's bed, according to newspaper and wildlife agency reports.

Fishing and tourist villages line the coast of the island that faces the Canadian mainland. Flower baskets hang from eaves, and highway signs invite passersby right into the homes of sculptors, potters, and weavers. One of those villages is Campbell River, where Karen Stevan and her partner were awakened one August morning at 1:00 A.M. as their house cat, Little Joe, came flying through the pet door. The cat was shivering and yowling, so they comforted him before going back to sleep. The next morning they found seven cougar-killed sheep in the pasture of the farm where they lived. Karen also discovered a deep scratch on her cat's back. Little Joe had apparently been very lucky indeed.

At the island's southern tip lies urbane, elegant Victoria, provincial capital of British Columbia and home to the most famous Vancouver Island cougar story of all.

It was mid-March of 1992 and Tim Loewen was minding the yellow cashier's booth in the Empress Hotel's underground parking garage. The TV was on and he was talking on the phone, so he barely noticed the car at the gate until the cabby honked. Tim cupped the receiver and slid open the window.

"You got a cougar in here," the cabby hollered, pointing down the ramp into the concrete cavern.

"What?" Loewen laughed.

The cabby was not laughing. "A cougar just walked into your parkade," he repeated.

The Empress is no rustic lodge in the woods. It's a seven-story castle in downtown Victoria where the bellmen dress in livery, the staff's manners are spot-on, and the best rooms start at one thousand dollars Canadian per night. A city block wide, it's the focal point of the teeming inner harbor. More than one hundred thousand pilgrims a year come for high tea at the Empress. Just as Queen Elizabeth once did, they poke out their pinkies, hoist a dainty china cup, and wait for the "Tea Mum" to serve a scone or some clotted cream.

A cougar at the Empress? Just in case, Tim rolled the security gate shut. Perhaps attracted by the noise, a big golden animal padded out of the gloom. Tim stared, astonished, as the graceful creature threw itself against the gate with an echoing crash.

Night manager David Woodward listened calmly to the voice on the phone blathering about a cougar trapped in the parking garage. Obviously some nervous part-timer had gotten himself spooked by a stray dog. Still, one had to take precautions. It wouldn't do to lose a hotel guest to a wild animal.

Feeling foolish, he dispatched bellmen to seal off all doors between the garage and the hotel. Then he went to see for himself. Two levels down, he and the valet van driver found a smartly dressed guest putting a bag in his car. A little drunk, the man laughed uproariously at Woodward's warning. A cougar among the Cadillacs? It sounded funny to Woodward too.

Moments later, Woodward leaned out the window to warn a woman rummaging in her trunk. She didn't laugh, though: He didn't get far past the word "cougar" before she slammed the lid and ran for the elevator. Woodward and the driver were still chuckling when something big glided through the van's headlights.

Fire? Woodward knew what to do. Earthquake? It was right there in the emergency procedure manual. Carnivore in your three-hundred-car garage? Not a clue.

Of all the principals in this story, conservation officer Bob Smirl was the only one unsurprised when the call came. He was relieved. For two days Bob had been fielding reports of a cougar sighted first in Victoria's suburbs, then deeper and deeper into the city. One of those reports had troubled him. The cat had walked right past a man cleaning his parking lot with a noisy high-pressure hose. The animal sounded far too bold for Smirl's tastes. He was glad it was finally penned up, even if the pen was the parking garage of the Empress Hotel.

Pulling up to the hotel, the first thing Smirl saw was perhaps two hundred people, including what looked like every television and newspaper reporter in town. Most were crowded around a steel security grate, peering into the garage.

Smirl carried a tranquilizer gun, his Plan A. His houndsman and a helper each held a tracking dog on a short leash. The houndsman was in charge of Plan B: a .30-30 Winchester carbine. Smirl could see distaste on faces in the crowd. He knew from experience their problem was with the gun. Somebody raised the gate, and Smirl and the others stepped inside. It closed behind them with a metallic crash.

"OK, now we're locked in here with this thing," Smirl thought. Outside, the crowd murmured. It sounded like they were rooting for the cougar.

The dogs seemed to strike fresh scent everywhere. They hauled their handlers forward, paws scrabbling at the cement. Their baying echoed through the cavernous parkade. Smirl eyed the rows of late-model luxury sedans.

"How am I going to explain bullet holes in these cars?" he wondered.

Moments later, the cougar stepped from behind a small car into their path. Ears back and eyes slitted, it crouched and began to belly-crawl toward the dogs.

The frantic hounds lunged for the cougar, forcing their handlers to lean back hard. Bob eased to the side. Intent on the dogs, the cat didn't notice him. Bob raised the dart gun. When the fluffy-tailed metal dart found the cat's hip, it spun fast, locking eyes with Bob. Bob raised the dart gun before his face and braced for impact. But the cougar whirled away, diving beneath an air duct. A second dart finished the job, knocking the cat unconscious.

The crowd cheered when Smirl and his helpers carried out the cougar, handcuffed in case it woke too soon. This was perfect PR, Smirl knew. Cougar stories ending with a game warden's bullet were not nearly as popular around Victoria as in the little bush towns up-island.

Smirl displayed the animal on his tailgate, showed the crowd its claws and teeth. He answered questions about how the cat would be returned to its world. Then he placed a towel over the cougar's head to make sure it stayed unaware, and fifty people filed by to touch it. One woman snuggled her face into its belly fur.

"Thank you," she told Smirl. "This is the most wonderful experience I've ever had."

Interviewed on national news, night manager Woodward joked that the cougar was a bit late for tea, and not properly attired for it anyway. A decade later, a picture still hung in the Empress's richly furnished lobby: a limp mountain lion being evicted from the hotel.

The Empress cougar made for a great story, especially if you sweep one inconvenient detail under the rug. As Smirl well knew, relocation is not "a wonderful experience" for the cougar. It's usually fatal.

———

Stories of cougars venturing deep into humanscapes were startling in 1992. They were less so by 1998, when another Vancouver Island cougar made news.

Craig Grebicki was a salesman for Scott Plastics, a fishing gear manufacturer. Overlooking Victoria's harbor, his office building was part of a crowded older neighborhood visible from the Empress. It was a hot fall afternoon, so someone had left the front door open for air.

As he was about to take a break from his phone, Craig thought he saw the tip of a long tail flash in the corner of his eye. Then an animal was rearing up, placing its paws on an interior windowsill. It was a cougar.

All that stood between them was a file cabinet and a potted plant. At first the animal ignored him. It dropped back to the floor and padded into another office. Through another window in the wall, they made eye contact for three long seconds. When the cougar turned away, Craig was ready: He shoved his chair into the doorway and sprinted for the back entrance. As the door slammed shut behind him, he heard something hit the other side with a thud.

In 1992, the year of the Empress cat, cougars attacked two people on Vancouver Island, one in a school playground. By the time Craig Grebicki slammed that door six years later, five more attacks had been reported.

But these occurrences were nothing new on Vancouver Island. The dramatic increase in attacks that the United States experienced in the 1990s had already occurred there in the 1950s.

Vancouver Islanders say attacks are more frequent on their island simply because their island has more cougars than anywhere else in the world. They say it with rueful relish, the way New Yorkers brag about their expensive rents.

It is probably true that the island's cougar population is unusually high. A research team on the east side of the island once counted three times as many cougars as is thought typical elsewhere in North America.

On Vancouver Island the balance is tipped in favor of the predator, says longtime conservation officer and cougar capture expert Gerry Brunham. The mild climate means that survival requires the expenditure of fewer calories. Coastal blacktail deer, the subspecies that inhabits the island, are smaller than mule deer or whitetail, presumably making them easier to kill. In addition, the island's lush vegetation favors the ambush hunter. Kittens and subadults have higher survival rates here, Gerry has heard.

But it's unlikely that lion density provides the whole answer. The Olympic peninsula of Washington state is also known to have high cougar populations, and yet its cougar conflicts began much more recently.

Renowned cougar researcher Maurice Hornocker once proposed that intensive hunting might have increased the proportion of aggressive cats on Vancouver Island. He noted that cougars are nearly always hunted with tracking hounds. Perhaps the shyest cougars tree fastest at the sound of baying hounds and are killed. Bolder cats elude the dogs or stay on the ground to fight and occasionally win both their lives and the chance to pass on those more aggressive skills or genes.

It is true that Vancouver Island houndsmen have killed a lot of cougars. In times past, when the goal was eradication, the take was as high as 460 cats per year. This is a staggering number when you consider that the highest cougar population the island has supported is probably around one thousand. After the advent of controlled sport hunting the kill number dropped, but hunters are still thought to kill about 15 percent of the island's cats every year.

If it's true that an island ecosystem, because it experiences no immigration, tends to concentrate the effects of change on the gene pool, Maurice Hornocker's old theory could be right on. Vancouver Island hunters may have spent the last century shaping a bolder, more aggressive cougar.

From the craggy roadside overlooks just north of Victoria, it appears as if the island's center is an undisturbed sanctuary of deep timber. But from the air, Vancouver Island is revealed as a checkerboard of clear-cuts. About half of the island has been logged. When a forest is first timbered, the grasses and shrubs once robbed of light begin to thrive. This young forest provides plentiful spring forage for deer and other species, but it's the dense canopy of old growth forest that provides winter protection. And after about thirty years the now nearly impenetrable second growth forest becomes a green desert choked with tough-leafed salal.

One result is that Vancouver Island deer numbers have varied wildly over the last fifty years. In the 1960s and 1970s, their numbers exploded until, by 1980, the population was estimated at a whopping 200,000. By 2001 it had fallen to 55,000, the lowest ever recorded. Roller-coaster change like that must have seismic repercussions for the deer's co-species, the cougar. Could competition over a dwindling food supply help produce a bolder cougar? Perhaps.

Especially if you add in another aspect of the island ecosystem: It lacks small prey. Matt Austin, the province's large-carnivore specialist, read a theory back in the early 1990s that made sense to him. The author, Paul Beier, postulated that the lack of rabbits, porcupines, coyotes, and skunks might contribute to a more aggressive cougar on Vancouver Island. An animal that has no choice but to hunt large game might necessarily be bolder, particularly during a human-caused die-back of its prey species.

It's also possible, says Gerry Brunham, that it's the habitat, not the cougars, which are responsible. He points out that the island's unusually dense vegetation means that cougars have only seconds to make up their minds to leap. Throughout much of the West, a cougar can watch an animal as long as it wishes before deciding to attack, but on Vancouver Island by the time it's in sight, the deer—or child—is already within striking distance.

Across cougar country it is thought that habituation may lead to conflict, including attacks. A cougar living along the urban interface or in a popular recreation area probably sees humans almost daily. Particularly if the area is unhunted—and most urban areas are—the experience is neutral. The cougar learns humans are not particularly to be avoided. Then one night he finds a dog in a backyard. The cougar enjoys an easy meal in a place redolent with human sign. This begins to create a positive association.

Eventually, the theory says, the cougar begins to look curiously at humans themselves.

This theory was proposed most recently in a book called *The Beast in the Garden*, which essentially said that the tolerant, environmentally conscious residents of Boulder, Colorado, created cougar-human conflict by welcoming deer and other wildlife into their town, and then by refusing to eliminate the cougars that followed.

On Vancouver Island, however, attacks do not occur in the south where most residents and all of the cities are located, points out Lance Sundquist, regional manager for the Conservation Officer service. Between 2000 and 2005, every cougar attack—seven in all—occurred up-island where presumably cougars would be far less habituated. Conservation officers around Victoria deal with a tremendous volume of pet and livestock depredation complaints, but there have been no attacks, says Lance.

As Gerry Brunham likes to say, when conditions change, animals change. The cougar that leaped through Eddie McLean's window in 1951 was shaped by a very different Vancouver Island from the one that exists today. New forces will shape the cougar of tomorrow. Vancouver Island's mild weather and lovely landscape draw more immigrants all the time, many of them city people more interested in coexisting with cougars than in hunting them. Meanwhile there are those last old-growth forests and the deer that rely upon them. How the logging companies decide to manage those forests will have repercussions for all the island's residents, two-legged and four.

KYLE MUSSELMAN, 1994

Carved into a forested Vancouver Island hillside overlooking the village of Gold River, Scout Lake subdivision could be any one of a thousand middle-class developments outside of Seattle, Dallas, or Denver. Sidewalks, streetlights, and molded gutters march alongside the asphalt with comforting propriety. New cars and speedboats wait in the carports of well-tended two-story homes. But this suburb's commuters don't make their morning drive to the nearest city—it's three hours away. They work in what Canadians call "the bush." Forest stretches from the edge of town in all directions, creating a human island in an ocean of trees.

May 9, 1994, dawned unusually sunny for spring on the north end of Vancouver Island. Cool air poured off the surrounding mountains. In a tidy yellow house midway along Donner Street, twelve-year-old Brad Musselman began the task of rousing his seven-year-old brother, who shared the basement with him. Kyle, who let gung-ho Brittany do more than her share of the chores, was also mostly willing to let Brad be boss. So as he was told, Kyle dressed in jeans, sneakers, and a checkered flannel shirt. In his pockets he hid a pair of tree-shaped car air fresheners he'd been carrying around for weeks. One was vanilla; the other, pine. Brad laughed every time Kyle explained he liked to smell fresh.

Brad herded Kyle upstairs for breakfast. As usual, Brittany, a year older than Kyle, was already up. Their father, John, a late-shift mechanic for one of the logging outfits that supplied the pulp mill, was making breakfast. Their mother, Joan, an EMT, was away at a logging camp on Quadra Island, accessible only by plane.

They ate looking out the bay window at miles of timber, the sole reason for this town and the source of its residents' jobs. Then they settled in front of the TV to watch the Mario Brothers "Hoo! Hoo!" through another episode. About 8:30 A.M. the two boys and their sister slung up their day packs, said a quick goodbye to their dad, and left for school. John went back to bed.

At the corner of Donner and Cala, they met Tony Olson and his older brother, Jamie.

Farther up Donner, where trees were rapidly refilling home lots that had never sold, a hundred-foot staircase ran down the forested hillside from Scout Lake subdivision to the school. Paved with railroad ties, gravel, and asphalt, it dropped three flights with long asphalt landings between. An alder thicket grew on either side of the eight-foot path. Just past the bottom step, Canadian Highway 28 turned into a gravel road. The school lay directly across the road.

Kyle and Tony's oversized backpacks bounced back and forth across their butts as they clattered down the stairs one landing ahead of Brad and Jamie. Brittany dawdled behind. When Tony called out a race and took off, Kyle shouted and chased after him.

A dark blur burst out of the alder thicket and flew after Kyle.

Stretched out in midair, the lunging animal seemed to Brad as long as the staircase was wide. Its front paws found Kyle's right shoulder. The impact spun Kyle around and slammed him onto his back, looking up into the jaws of the golden animal that completely covered him.

"Holy shit, it's a cougar," Brad said.

Kyle began screaming in short, high-pitched bursts. He kicked at the cat's belly and tried to push its jaws away with small hands.

Tony Olsen had stopped when he heard Kyle's first screams. Now he was throwing rocks at the cat. Brad didn't bother with rocks. They needed an adult. With his brother still screaming on the ground, Brad sprinted for home.

John woke the moment the door banged. As he struggled from bed, he heard Brad's voice, cracking as it rose. "Dad, hurry Kyle's being attacked."

On autopilot John scooped up a pair of Levi shorts from the floor and plunged down the stairs two at a time. He came up short when he realized he didn't know where he was rushing to or why.

"Dad, hurry up, he's being eaten by a cougar!"

"What?" John snapped back, finally and fully realizing that he was staring at only two of his three children. "Where?"

Brad and Brittany's eyes were huge. "On the stairwell! Hurry up!"

The top of the stair was three hundred paces from his door. John ran barefoot up the street. He could see the staircase, but he wasn't getting there fast enough.

"Oh my god, a cougar. This isn't really happening."

John had hunted and hiked the hills of British Columbia all his life, and he had never seen a cougar in the wild. Paved, suburban Donner Street was nothing like the muddy trail to school he'd walked as a boy on the mainland. Yet here he was, running past the doctor's house and the piano teacher's living room—to face a cougar. All he could hear were his feet slapping the pavement and the tapping toenails of Kyle's little lap dog, Dexter, scampering along behind him.

When he grabbed the railing and made the turn onto the staircase, he saw a neighbor, Ingrid Dahl, on the landing below. She was hurling a fist-sized rock into the alders beside the stairs.

After the kids ran past her house screaming, Ingrid had watched another neighbor run inside for a phone. She didn't know what had happened but she understood this: A child was alone down there with some awful kind of trouble.

Dressed in slippers and her husband's blue bathrobe, she had hurried to the top of the staircase. Seeing no one, she had called out, "Where are you?"

Far below a clump of alders began whipping. She eased down the steps, slowed by her imagination but determined to do something.

John pounded down the stairs. "Where is he?" he demanded as he reached the landing. "Where is he?" He ran in the direction Ingrid pointed, toward the now quiet alder thicket.

John crouched, peering into the green shadows until he spotted Kyle's sneakers. He bent closer. His eyes moved methodically from the boy's feet to his legs. No motion. Kyle lay on his stomach. As John crawled closer, something inexplicable happened: The boy's body slithered away, rippling like water over rocks. John watched, dumbfounded, as Kyle's feet bounced up a leafy tunnel, coming to a stop twenty feet away. Forcing his eyes upward, John saw that Kyle's arced-up back and twisted neck were being held off the ground by a cougar. Its jaws were closed over Kyle's face, so that cougar and boy were mouth to mouth.

The cat was crouched slightly to the left of Kyle's body. Hanging from Kyle's bloody white skull was most of his scalp, a wet mop coated with leaves and dirt. Kyle had to be gone. John and the cougar locked eyes.

"You son of a bitch," John muttered. He glared harder. So did the cat. A long moment passed and then John suddenly boiled with fury. "Get off him!" he roared.

The cat flinched but didn't drop the body. Instead, it hunkered even lower. John charged, intending to either retrieve his son or dive in beside him.

"Get off him!" he shouted again. The last shout seemed to break the cat's trance. Just as John closed the gap, the cat dropped Kyle and leapt, but not at John. Instead it sailed four feet above his outstretched arms.

The cougar landed, spun, and dashed into the bush. John yelled again to make sure it kept moving. Then he turned to his son.

Kyle was lying facedown with his arms outstretched like a crucifix. John could see slick, bloody bone on the crown of Kyle's head. At the base of the skull was a little tuft of unbloodied blonde hair and then the sweet pale skin of his neck. Supporting the neck the way he'd been taught in first-aid classes, he turned the boy over. At the sight of Kyle's face, he gasped and nearly dropped him, bobbling the head and shoulder in his hands.

The face was all blood and raw flesh. Only the tip of a nose remained. The bridge was gone. John could see into the nasal cavity. Both cheeks were shredded. One eyeball was deflated, the ear on that side ripped. John couldn't find any sign of the little boy whose face had crumpled into tears two weeks before when he'd questioned him about goofing around with those damn air fresheners.

"Oh, my God," John breathed. Dexter shouldered in beside him, trying to nuzzle the boy. John shoved him away.

Then a little bubble of blood formed where the boy's mouth should have been. John snapped to attention.

"Kyle!" he called out sharply. "Hang in there! Kyle, it's Daddy! Breathe! Breathe, Kyle! Just breathe! Don't worry about anything, just breathe!"

Standing up, John made his way toward the path, trying with one hand to throw Kyle's scalp back up on his head when it caught on branches.

"Kyle, breathe. Do nothing but breathe." He didn't know what Kyle could hear, but it made him feel better to say it.

Then he stopped. Kyle had said something. John was sure of it.

"What?"

"Who are you?" It came faint and quiet, as if it took all the boy's effort.

"Kyle? . . . Daddy! Just hang in there."

Hope hit him hard. All those head wounds, yet Kyle had spoken.

"Kyle, are you OK?" he asked.

"No," whimpered the boy inside the mash of blood and bone. "No."

"Just hang in there, Kyle. You're going to be OK. Don't do anything but breathe."

His across-the-street neighbor, Glen McNichol, practically ran into them as John emerged from the bush. In one hand, Glen carried a home-made knife the size of a machete.

"He's alive," John said. The men ran toward the school.

In the teachers' parking lot, a red Ford minivan was easing into place. The driver looked up when John yelled for help.

"Open the back door," teacher Carol Volk told her daughter. "You don't have to look. A child is hurt."

John cradled Kyle as they drove, repeating over and over: "I'm here. . . . Hang on, I'm here with you. . . . Breathe."

He burst into the Gold River clinic with Kyle in his arms. "Cougar attack, cougar attack! He's alive!" he shouted.

"Do you want these back?" a nurse asked as she cut off Kyle's bloody shirt and pants and untied his sneakers. "No," John said, shaking his head. "What's he weigh?" the doctor asked, calculating a sedative dose. John had no idea.

A Bowater Paper Company helicopter arrived to take Kyle to the hospital in Campbell River, an hour away by car.

"If you want to do anything for Daddy, breathe," John commanded as they were loading Kyle into the chopper. "Breathe."

As the pilot prepared to lift off, he shot a thumbs-up at John who shot one back. John had gotten to Kyle in time, and the boy was breathing just like he'd been told. Now that he was in expert hands, the worst was over. The helicopter lifted off and one of the doctors, a next-door neighbor, drove John home to get cleaned up and dressed for the trip to Campbell River.

In his bathroom, John left bloody fingerprints on everything he touched. He turned on the shower and pulled off his shorts. "Oh, Jeez, what a mess," he said as he pulled back the shower curtain. "Holy Christ, what a mess." The walls of the shower ran red.

While Kyle was still at the clinic, Glen McNichol ran to the other end of Gold River's government campus, long knife still in hand, and found Royal Canadian Mounted Police Constable Rick McKerracher. The two went to the stairs and almost immediately spotted a cougar. It crouched and bared its teeth, all the proof the men needed. McKerracher killed it with a shot to the head. They carried the carcass to the RCMP office, where McKerracher posed with it for newspaper photos that flashed across Canada the next day.

John hurriedly packed a bag. He muttered in frustration, patting his pockets. He had no cash.

"Don't leave, Dad," Brad said. "Hang on a minute."

Puffing back up the stairs from his basement bedroom, Brad handed John a small wad of bills. John hadn't cried when he found Kyle face-down and motionless. He'd kept his cool at the clinic and as he'd watched the helicopter take his boy away. But now, holding Brad's savings, he felt the tears come. He pulled Brad close and held on.

At the hospital in Campbell River John was ushered into a cold operating room full of instruments and rolling dollies. Two staffers huddled off to one side. Kyle lay motionless under a gauze drape with the operating light beating down on him. His Tasmanian Devil underwear was lying in the trash. John stopped short. There was no one tending his boy.

John didn't breathe again until someone explained that Kyle was alive, but needed the skills of big-city surgeons. John had seen that torn little face and realized they were right. They were flying him to Children's Hospital in Vancouver. John held Kyle's hand and talked to him, telling him to just think about breathing. The little white fingers pressed lightly against John's hard palm.

Joan arrived in time to fly to Vancouver with John. They reached Children's Hospital around 1:00 P.M. At 3:00 P.M. the surgery began. Hospital staff told them to go get settled at the Easter Seals house for parents of young patients. The operation was expected to last fourteen hours.

They were back at the hospital by 4:00 A.M. At about 7:00 A.M. the plastic surgeon came to the private room where they waited. Doctor Nancy Van Laeken pulled off her surgical cap and sat in a heavy upholstered chair next to John and Joan. Tall, slim, and attractive, she was still in surgical booties and scrubs. She looked tired.

"I can't believe he's alive," she told them. But they needed to forget any hopes that they'd see Kyle's old face again. The doctor said she had several pieces of his cheekbone on ice. Some of those pieces might be refitted in later surgeries. She spelled out the options for face and scalp reconstruction and walked them through the process of installing a glass eye.

"You're very lucky to still have him," she said.

This was much worse than John had expected. Kyle had spoken, answered questions. Didn't that mean he'd be fine? John tried to pay attention. Now Dr. Van Laeken was describing the wires that were holding Kyle's face together.

Shock, the body shutting down organs in response to blood loss and dehydration, was the next threat, another doctor said. Doctors also warned that animal bites can cause lethal infections. John stiffened at the realization that Kyle was still in danger.

Finally they called John and Joan to see their boy.

"He looks so good," said a smiling nurse who stopped them along the way.

John looked anxiously around. The last time he had been in a big hospital, Kyle was a premature baby in a tidy neonatal care unit. This wide-open intensive-care ward looked like a war zone. It was crowded with whispering doctors and nurses, urgently tending to motionless patients buried in tubes and beeping machines. This wasn't a broken bone and stitches ward, it was a heart attack, bleed-to-death, burned-to-death ward.

John and Joan slowed when they reached Kyle's bed. The puffy face lay on a white pillow. Countless stitches pulled against the swelling, purple flesh. When Joan saw Kyle's face, she turned back to John, hand to her mouth. He realized she hadn't had any idea what the cougar had done. Kyle had already been wrapped in gauze when she'd reached Campbell River. He could feel his strong wife struggle and then give in to her tears, shaking and sobbing against his chest.

But John was smiling. Kyle was plugged into beeping machines like everyone else in the room. He had tubes in his throat and feet, and stitches all over. But John had seen worse when he rolled Kyle over in the bush. Through all the stitches and swelling bruises, he could see his son again.

"Oh my God," he thought, realizing he'd been right all along. "He's going to be OK."

6

GOLD RIVER

Viewed from the air, the Gold River Valley seems all forest and fjord, a temperate jungle often misty with remnants of rain and the exhalations of millions of conifers. Clear-cuts scar nearly every mountainside, but mostly the senses are struck by riotous growth from underbrush to overstory.

The town of Gold River didn't grow naturally. It was built all at once in 1965 to the specifications of the Tahsis Paper Company, which was installing a huge new pulp mill on the nearby river delta. The company needed about two thousand people to run the mill, including loggers, engineers, technicians, and laborers, and these people needed homes. Laid out in tidy grids with a pedestrian shopping mall at its center, even thirty years later Gold River looked like a movie set on which the paint was still drying.

If it sounds idyllic, it was. But what Gold River had forgotten is that here, more even than most human places, the line between town and bush is about as meaningful as the stripes of a painted cattle guard. Streets, streetlights, and sidewalks mark the edge of town for humans, but bears and cougars aren't as governed by such artificial boundaries.

Months after the youngest Musselman boy was attacked by a cougar on his way to school, Gold River was still trying to recover from its rude awakening. But on the sunny day when Kyle came home, the town confronted a more painful lesson: Some events can leave a person, or a town, forever changed.

A kid-painted welcome poster hung over the city limits sign where a police escort waited. The clapping and cheering began before John and Joan's van turned onto Donner Street. Balloons and streamers lashed in the breeze, and the bright shiny sound of children's voices filled the street.

Riding high in the front seat, Kyle waved to the crowd. As the van pulled up to his house, he spotted his best friend, Johnny Watts, who'd sent tape-recorded letters to the hospital. Kyle swung the van door open and stepped down, smiling.

Johnny's mother, Denise, stared. Before the attack Kyle had been a little chubby. Now he was emaciated. Only one side of his face moved as he continued to bravely smile into the ring of staring faces. Bright pink scars traced the path of claws through his right eye and forehead. His nose was off-center and that eyelid drooped over a dark implant. He wore a bandana on his head, but it couldn't hide the fact that he had little hair left. All Denise could see was a small tuft below his ears. It all looked so painful.

Johnny, who had been dancing with excitement, froze. Kyle walked to him through the crowd.

"Hi, John," he said.

Johnny turned and ran.

Denise caught up with him on the highway. "That's not Kyle," Johnny wailed. "It's got his voice, but it's not his face."

Kyle not only looked different, but he had also lost the verve that had made him a favorite around town. He jumped anytime someone crushed a sheet of paper or rattled a plastic food wrapper. It sounded like the cougar moving in the brush, he said.

Gold River didn't look different at all, but it too was changed. Gone was the naïve assurance that a town could, by appearing neat, secure, and rational, exempt itself from the bush and the dangers that might wander out of it.

Now what? How could the town feel secure again? A few obvious steps had immediately presented themselves. The morning of the attack, Dale Frame walked down to the staircase from his house in Scout Lake subdivision. There he found Glen McNichol, whom he knew from the mill. Glen had an idea. They would cut back the alder thicket. Then another cat would not be able to lie unseen three feet from the path. By noon, he and Glen had parked their pickups at the top of the stairs and unloaded chainsaws. Dale yanked a starter cord and set to work. His saw wailed and threw bone-white dust.

He had moved to Gold River when it was little more than a bull-dozed clear-cut at the end of the highway. The cougars had always been around, but as the trees grew back, the deer had come too. And the deer lured the cougars closer. You couldn't blame the cougar, Frame planned to remind people. The animal had been young and hungry, presented with an easy meal and perfect ambush cover. It knew neither right nor wrong, only opportunity and the simple calculus of life: A kill meant food, and food meant survival.

That ambush cover was vanishing fast. Within an hour the project had attracted a crowd. Ax-wielding mothers were hacking off low branches at the clearing's edge. People looked serious and worried as reports came in from the hospital. Critical condition. Respirators. Surgery.

The staircase looked good with a haircut. For the first time in years, you could stand at the top and see all the way to the bottom.

Parents met later the same week with Pat Brown-Clayton, Gerry Brunham, and Knut Atkinson from the Ministry of Environment. A little boy had almost been killed. The town wanted to hear what the ministry would do to prevent another attack.

There would be no wholesale cougar hunt, they were told, and nothing short of that would make much difference. Scout Lake subdivision lay in the ancient migration trails of game animals, Brown-Clayton said. Having built your town in a river bottom in the bush, you'd have to expect wild animals to pass through and occasionally do unpredictable things. Attacks are awful, the game wardens agreed. But they are also incredibly rare. You can't kill all the cougars because of one freak event. The Ministry of Environment's job is to protect wildlife, not wipe it out. Besides, the cougar whose error it had been to attack a human child had died for its mistake. The child was alive.

None of that was comforting, some said, not if you'd seen John Musselman running across the highway with a bloody bundle in his arms.

A line of cars began showing up at the schoolyard every morning and afternoon. People who had chosen Gold River as a place to raise their kids away from busy traffic and dangerous strangers were now driving their kids to school, just as they would have in the big cities they had fled. Some residents kicked around a plan to fire up a siren any time a cougar was sighted. They looked for cougar repellant to spread around town and talked about building a fence down both sides of what kids were now calling the Cougar Stairs. But as others pointed out, no one had seen Kyle's cougar before the attack, so a siren wouldn't have helped. There is no such thing as a permanent cougar repellant; and the fences would just force traveling bears and cougars up into Scout Lake subdivision or down into the schoolyard by cutting off a densely wooded corridor.

John Musselman came home to Gold River angry. He'd grown up in a logging family on the mainland where sightings of cougars were rare, and those that were seen were glimpsed as they timidly darted from sight. But these cats around Gold River were not afraid of people, John told reporters. There were weeks in which a cougar was sighted in town every day. People were so scared they wouldn't let their kids play outside or walk three blocks to the store, John said.

Less than a week after they brought Kyle home, John and Joan were out for an evening walk when their dog started barking its head off. John walked over to investigate and found himself face to face with another cougar. Clearly there were too many. Every cougar that came to town should be shot. He failed to see how any right-minded person would think otherwise.

For a time, John still suffered screaming nightmares of the bloody hash of Kyle's head. But day by day, as he watched Kyle go to school without hiding his scars and muster the courage to ride his bike and play hockey one-eyed, John too felt stronger.

The nightmares faded. His anger cooled. He slowly eased into line with those who accepted the risk. He drove the kids to school when he could and forbade them to take the staircase shortcut when he couldn't. But he also began saying, "You can't kill everything off just because you're afraid of them and there's been an accident. It's one of them things in life. . . . You know, it happens."

Bonnie Bellwood accepted the slim risk, too. Four years after Kyle's attack, her older kids were among the few who still walked to school alone and played in the bush as kids had done for thirty years in Gold River.

September 4, 1998, dawned sunny and warm for a fall day on the north end of Vancouver Island. In her house at 420 Donner Street, Bonnie roused her twelve-year-old son, Brandon, her nine-year-old daughter, Britney, and her kindergartner, Chelsea. Awake and finally moving, Chelsea dressed in black lace-up boots, black leggings, and a pink fleece sweatshirt. Breakfast was toast and peanut butter, served by her mum, who gently bossed the kids along. As usual, Britney left first with a friend. Brandon left when he wouldn't have to be seen with Britney. Then Chelsea slung up her pink and white cartoon backpack, grabbed her mother's hand and headed out the door. The hundred-foot staircase that connects the subdivision to the schoolyard was just two doors up the street.

Wearing a pink housecoat and flip-flops, Bonnie stopped at the top of the stairs and kissed Chelsea goodbye.

"Watch crossing the road and go right to your class," she said as the little girl trudged down the stairs.

"Bye, Mom," Chelsea said.

She took a few steps and turned around, "See ya later, Mom."

Chelsea was nearly at the bottom when Bonnie first saw the bear. Big and black, it stepped onto the path beside the girl. Chelsea looked tiny as she spun around to look for her mom. Even at that distance Bonnie thought she could see her daughter's wide eyes through her glasses.

Bonnie couldn't make a sound. She ran four steps toward her child, then stopped, afraid to aggravate the bear. She backed up to the top and hated that, too. She imagined herself yelling, "Chelsea, come here now!" but that didn't seem right, either.

As she'd been taught in cougar safety lessons at school, Chelsea hollered and put her hands above her head. Then, confused, she crouched down as if to hide.

The bear looked at the little girl but kept walking. It pooped out two eight-inch-long scats purple with fall berries. They steamed on the blacktop as the bear shambled out of the logged zone and into the forest. Bonnie ran down and Chelsea scrambled into her arms.

"I was playing invisible," she said as they climbed back to the street at the top of the stairs.

They waited there for a minute and then walked to school together. Bonnie thought hard about her decision to let her children walk the Cougar Stairs and play in the woods. Some parents wouldn't let their kids play at her house because of it. But she knew that Kyle's attack four years before had been a fluke, just as Chelsea's encounter now was a fluke. Bonnie's kids were as safe today as they'd been all the years Gold River's other kids ran carefree about town.

Nevertheless, at noon she drove down and picked Chelsea up for lunch. The school had been rebuilt since Kyle's attack, but the same queue of parents lined up at the new building's front doors as had appeared there the day he was mauled.

"I could have petted him, mum," the little girl said.

"No joke, Chels. You could have rode him."

Bonnie picked Chelsea up again at the end of the day.

7

THE RESEARCHERS

The young cougar had recently won his seventy-five-square-mile territory in New Mexico's San Andres Mountains. Now, ears and lips tacked back in a futile snarl, left front leg caught in a loop of cable, he stared at his captors through narrowed amber eyes.

Biologist Linda Sweanor and the research team stayed cautiously out of range, waiting for the tranquilizing dart to do its work. Within a few moments, Linda was crouching over a semi-conscious cat. His eyes were open, but he seemed glassily blind to the humans' presence. Knocking him out completely would have been safer for the researchers but riskier for the cat. A heavily drugged animal has a harder time maintaining body temperature, and as it is recovering, is an easy target for predators.

The team worked efficiently, slipping the snare from the heavy leg, measuring and weighing. The cat was beautifully fit and, at 145 pounds, large for a desert cougar. They tattooed an identifying mark in one ear, clipped a plastic tag to the other, and encircled his neck with a battery-operated, one-pound radio collar. It made his neat, round head appear even smaller, incongruous on the big body stretched before them. Their receivers would be able to hear the collar's signal from miles away. Linda was pleased to note that one of the cat's toes, once broken, jutted from his right forefoot at a distinctive angle: It would give him a signature track.

Wildlife researchers try not to get sentimental about their subjects, so they labeled more than named him. Since he was the third cat Linda and her colleagues had snared for this study, he would be called Male 3.

The year was 1985. Linda and her new husband Kenny Logan, the project lead, were just beginning the most intensive long-term cougar study ever attempted. The project would run year-round for a decade, eventually involving eight researchers and 294 cougars scattered across the San Andres Mountains, a rugged and remote eighty-mile-long range in the Chihuahuan Desert. Linda would follow Male 3's radio signal and broken-toed track, in small planes and on foot, living in tents and trailers, for nine of those ten years.

While this kind of dedication is not uncommon among field researchers, for those who study the elusive cougar it's almost required. Yet despite four decades of committed research, many basic questions about the species remain unanswered. Researchers don't know, for instance, how wild cougar kittens play or what the probably tense encounters between adults look like. How do cougar mothers teach kittens to hunt? Do families hunt cooperatively? Nobody knows, because nobody gets to watch.

There are lucky exceptions, like the time Montanan Tom Parker found a dead white-tailed deer down the road from his house. Tom is a professional tracker who works with researchers. He knew he'd found a cougar kill, and a recent one. He contacted a friend who owned a fancy video camera. The two set it up and left. The resulting tape shows an adult female and two or possibly three kittens visiting the kill one at a time. Each comes in silently, feeds for a few minutes, then steps back, chirps like a bird, and leaves. After a few minutes another silently appears and begins to feed, only to get up in a little while, chirp, and leave.

Is this a typical feeding scene? Nobody knows.

Nevertheless, radio-collar studies are the best tool researchers have to unlock the cougar's secrets. They work like this: Researchers select an area within which, ideally, they will try to collar every cougar. If the study can afford them (top of the line collars cost as much as five thousand dollars each), they will buy collars that use both GPS (global positioning system) and old-fashioned radio VHF (very high frequency) technology. The

GPS unit records the animal's location at regular intervals. But in order to retrieve that data, the researchers still need to locate the collar or the cat, and that requires the collar's VHF signal.

In the mid-1980s, GPS technology was not yet available. So for the New Mexico study, each of many thousands of cougar locations had to be recorded manually by a researcher pinpointing a cat's unique VHF radio signal. These signals are nothing more than staticky beeps that vary in speed and intensity depending upon the cat's position. In rugged country, they can bounce about like echoes, sending researchers trudging up a mountain's flank even while the subject sleeps in a thicket below.

Biologists have traditionally captured cats for collaring according to a method pioneered by researcher Maurice Hornocker in the 1960s. Once fresh tracks are found—by far, the most time-consuming part of cat hunting—an experienced houndsman releases his dogs on the scent. Most cougars chased by hounds quickly tree, a fact which makes this method relatively safe for all involved. In the nearly treeless desert of the New Mexico study, however, dogs would have caught the cougars on the ground, a recipe for bloodshed on both sides. A solution came from woodsman and trapper Frank Smith, who had killed perhaps three hundred cats for sport or as part of his job as a New Mexico depredation control officer. Smith taught the Hornocker researchers about leghold snares.

The researchers learned to place snares along an animal's favorite travel paths, and to position obstacles around a camouflaged snare to lead the animal's foot onto the spring-loaded trigger plate. Cougars prefer to eat their own kills but will sometimes scavenge, especially fresh deer meat. So traps were set around a cougar's kill when one could be found, or around road-killed deer that the researchers placed along a favorite travel route. Averaged over time, it took 193 "snare-days" (one snare in place for one day) to catch one cougar. Nevertheless the team eventually radio collared 126 cougars, including broken-toed Male 3.

Since the 1960s, when as a young Ph.D. candidate Maurice Hornocker undertook the first intensive radio-collar cougar study, patient biologists like Linda Sweanor have accumulated a surprising amount of information about this secretive carnivore. For instance, despite the fact that even in the heart of cougar country a cougar sighting is a remarkable thing, we know the species is no longer rare. California estimates its cougar population at 4000 to 6000. Nevada estimates it has 3000 to 4000, New Mexico about 2150. Cougars spread themselves thinly across habitat, so although these numbers are small, it's believed they generally represent healthy, sustainable populations.

Nor are there necessarily too many cougars, as many have assumed based on increases in cougar sightings and cougar-human conflicts. Researchers in the Pacific Northwest recently set their sights on understanding a population of cougars assumed to be expanding based on a local increase in cougar-human encounters. Hunter quotas had been raised to curb this undesirable population boom. The researchers found that, while intensive hunting was an effective population control—92 percent of mortality in study animals was due to hunters—it was perhaps too effective. The cougar population was declining. If the trend continued, that population of cougars could be expected to fade from existence in twenty-six years.

Another thing researchers have learned is how misleading that old chestnut "the balance of nature" can be. In natural systems the trend is always toward balance, but it is not necessarily the balance we would choose, nor is it a balance ever achieved.

In order to study how that trend toward balance occurs among cougars, the San Andres researchers simulated a sudden die-back. They removed most of the cougars from one area, relocating them hundreds of miles away. At first the remaining cats repopulated rapidly—cougar populations can increase at rates better than 25 percent a year—but as the population approached its original level, growth slowed to about 5 percent.

Then, by coincidence, drought struck. For three years in a row, deer populations declined. Poor forage weakened the remaining deer, concentrating them at the few reliable water sources. And lion numbers, rather than scaling back with decreasing deer numbers, increased. The result? Cougars helped push deer numbers down even faster, hastening their own eventual crisis.

In Montana, Erik Wenum found that when his region's deer population was reduced by 50 percent one harsh winter, cougars that spring initially thrived off the ready supply of weakened or dead deer. Females barely out of kittenhood produced young. A year later those surplus young were inexperienced hunters trying to compete with savvy adults for the few remaining deer. Those young animals began to starve. Although cougar numbers were plummeting, missing pet notices and problem cougar complaints in and around Kalispell went through the roof, sparking pressure to increase cougar hunting quotas.

Several mechanisms keep lions spread thinly on the land, shielding them from prey fluctuations. Depending on food supply, an adult female's territory might be twenty-five square miles while an adult male's can be more than a hundred. And while territories do overlap, radio collar studies show that adult cougars actively avoid one another except to mate, even if it means restructuring their territories.

Young cougars are left by their mothers after eleven to eighteen months in her care. Presumably confused, perhaps afraid, they may wait weeks for her return. But eventually they begin to wander. Some females and nearly all males leave the area in which they were born. On their journey they gain the adult size and skills that will allow them to hold territory of their own. Only the smartest and most cautious survive this rite of passage.

Dispersal is a powerful tool for the species' survival. When cougars in one area are dying, young dispersers can augment that failing population. In fact, geneticists believe that cougars disappeared from North America some ten thousand years ago. They don't know how this happened, but they do think that animals from Central America dispersed northward to repopulate the entire continent.

It is a human tendency to view small fluctuations in the balance of nature as imbalance, and assume human intervention is required to restore balance. When human hunters become less successful filling their deer tags, game agencies receive complaints that not enough predators, particularly cougars, are being killed. One reason cougars were bountied in the first place was their taste for deer flesh. Researchers estimate that adult cougars, given the opportunity, kill one deer every seven to fourteen or more days. That can sound like a lot of killing.

It is also true that cougars will kill more than they need, particularly when prey is vulnerable or can't escape—penned sheep, for instance.

Called surplus killing, this apparent wastefulness is partly how cougars earned their centuries' old reputation for wanton destruction. A single cougar will kill dozens of domestic sheep in a night, or bring down several deer within a few hundred yards of each other, or decimate a stressed population of endangered bighorn sheep.

You often hear that cougars kill the old and weak, that they improve a herd's health the way a careful gardener prunes to strengthen his trees. At a glance this would seem untrue. Studies have found that cougars often target fawns. They also kill big bucks, probably because bucks are more frequently alone. It is vulnerability in any form, not just sickness or old age, that makes a particular deer attractive as prey.

But from a species survival perspective, the most important segment of a deer population are the does, not the bucks or even the fawns. The lion, by targeting vulnerability, leaves that segment of the population alone.

The upshot is this: Under normal circumstances cougars do not limit deer herds. What impacts deer numbers most are pervasive events like heavy winter snows, drought, or habitat lost to human encroachment. A heavily hunted cougar population—and most are—is not being managed to serve "the balance of nature." It is simply a population in constant crisis and recovery.

Researchers have become increasingly aware that it's risky to over-generalize about the members of any species. With mountain lions this is even more true. Mountain lions are highly individual. Some cougars engage in surplus killing. Others don't. Most tree when chased by baying hounds. A few don't. Most strongly prefer deer when deer are available. A few mow through precious remnant herds of bighorn sheep.

Populations of cougars also vary. On average cougars are larger in the North and smaller in the South. In some places, cougars frequently kill each other. In others, they don't. Some cougars, like those on Vancouver Island, seem more willing to behave aggressively toward humans. Cougars in Arizona—and no place else—regularly kill cattle. In that state, a typical cougar might eat more beef than venison. Cats elsewhere have the opportunity to kill cattle, but they mostly refrain.

And just as populations of cougars vary, so does each cougar population over time. "A cougar in the 1950s may not be the same type of animal as a cougar in 2006. Hunting affects them. Everything affects them. The survivors act differently. That's how they've survived," says Gerry Brunham, retired capture expert for Vancouver Island.

An idea called the Big Tom Theory argues that traditional cougar hunting can change cougar populations in ways that actually serve to increase cougar-human conflict. When a territorial male is killed, several subadults who would normally have dispersed divide the dead cat's territory, increasing the number of young cats that can live in that area. This matters because young animals are involved in a disproportionate number of cougar complaints, particularly those involving pet depredation.

California has not allowed sport hunting since 1972. There, generations of cougars have lived free of hunting pressure except for those killed on problem cougar permits. If hunting destabilizes cougar populations and leads to conflict, you might expect California to be a fairly peaceful place as far as cougars go. It's not. The state has recorded more attacks than any cougar region except British Columbia. Hunting advocates point to California as proof that cougars must be hunted to keep people safe. But the area with more cougar problems than California is Vancouver Island, where cougars have been hunted intensively since settlement.

In order to appreciate the rest of Male 3's story, you need to know that cougar's lives are precarious, so precarious that simply moving them to a new place is enough to tip the scales against them. Relocated cougars do have a chance, but it's slim, particularly for territorial adults who have spent their lives learning how to survive in their territories.

A sad story comes from Montana where, in 1997, a female and nearly grown kitten were relocated after attacking a dog in Glacier National Park. At capture both she and her kitten were healthy. The female weighed 120 pounds. A month later she killed a cocker spaniel and dragged it under a trailer in the nearby town of Essex. She was shot by wildlife officers. At her death she weighed eighty pounds. Her kitten, nowhere to be found, had probably already starved.

Male 3 stands out in Linda Sweanor's memory for one simple reason. He did what only very smart, very lucky cougars do: He survived. Male 3 was recaptured four times during the New Mexico study for recollaring; and each time he was healthy and strong. The researchers know that, at least once, he fought another adult male over a female. He won. The other male died.

He was middle-aged when Frank and the scientists set out to snare him one more time.

This time, the capture wasn't about battery replacement. The researchers wanted to use the cougars removed for the simulated die-back to document the harsh effects of relocation, still commonly used. Male 3 was among those slated for relocation.

The researchers tried for six months to trap him. They set snares along his travel routes. He stepped around them. Frank suggested they set two snares, one obvious and one hidden, so that a cat dealing with the first would step in the second. Male 3 sprang both, got caught in neither.

One day while setting snares near a kill surrounded by Male 3's big, jut-toed tracks, Linda looked up to see the patriarch himself staring at her. A frozen second passed; then he turned, tail-tip twitching, and glided away. When she was sure he was gone, she laid her snares.

Linda returned the next day to find she had finally won: Male 3 was caught. Then she realized that the cougar spitting and snarling at her was too small. It was a young male who'd snuck in to examine the kill. It's impossible to know what Male 3 made of this series of events, but the big cat abruptly stopped returning to any kill site the researchers had visited.

They finally gave up. They had removed fourteen animals from the test area. Male 3 remained. They monitored his movements, exasperated and a little admiring, as he took advantage of the unintended gift, expanding his territory until it encompassed nearly all the vacated ones.

Meanwhile they watched the relocated animals via their radio collars. Nine of the fourteen died. Eight attempted to return home, each traveling more than eighty kilometers in that direction. Two made it all the way back, one in about five months, the other in more than a year. One of these two males was able to reestablish his territory and survived. The other had already been usurped by Male 3. He began wandering again and died.

When a collared cougar is immobile for a period of time, usually six hours, a mercury switch in his collar trips and the transmission changes. Researchers call it a mortality signal. One day in 1994, Linda picked up a mortality signal on Male 3. Saddened, she hiked toward the source. The researchers were nearly at their project's conclusion. It would have been nice to pack up the tents and radio gear, the data charts and maps, knowing the wily old cougar was still out there on the desert.

But the signal had been accurate: Male 3 was dead. Examining the big cat made Linda feel better, though. He was perhaps thirteen, luxuriously old for a wild cougar. There was fur in his mouth, and mule deer liver and kidney in his belly. His fresh kill sprawled before him. He had died, full of fire and a fine meal, simply of old age. Of the 294 cougars Linda and her colleagues had studied during those ten years, only four were tough enough and smart enough to earn that peaceful death.

8

RONALD CASPERS WILDERNESS PARK, 1986

Sue Small turned around.

"Laura?"

Standing alone in the stream, Sue thought for a moment she'd imagined it: A flash of brown that grabbed her five-year-old by the head and climbed the bank, the child's small hands prying at its jaws. Now there was only the clucking of the stream, a few bugs buzzing and the smell of slow water on a warm day.

"Laura!"

It was March of 1986. Sue and her husband Don had driven into the foothills of Southern California's Santa Ana Mountains with Laura and their nine-year-old, David. Interstate 5 had been crowded with people headed to nearby San Juan Capistrano's annual Swallow Day celebration.

At the gate to Ronald Caspers Wilderness Park, which the family visited regularly, they were given the official map. It warned visitors of the most dangerous form of life in the park: poison oak.

The Smalls hiked north on a popular nature trail to San Juan Creek, where Sue and Laura took off their shoes to hold hands and wade in the shallows. Father and son soon grew bored and headed a little farther up the canyon.

"Why don't you go over to the edge of the stream and see if you can see the tadpoles now?" Sue told Laura, letting go of her hand. She watched her little girl, in white shorts and a blue tank top with butterflies on it, slosh away through ankle-deep water. As Laura bent to dip her plastic cup in the stream, Sue thought she saw something move at the edge of her vision. She turned, looking for a dog. What she saw was a cougar. A cougar? Before she could react, Laura was gone.

Sue called Laura's name again, struggling to disbelieve the awful image: Her baby had not, had absolutely not just been snatched by a wild animal. When the child didn't answer the third time, Sue believed. She screamed so hard she bent over with her hands on her knees to empty her lungs.

Don and David reappeared.

"A mountain lion has Laura. I don't know where they are," Sue yelled at them, and they were gone.

Sue splashed to the bank. Her penny loafers lay next to Laura's tiny sneakers. Reality slipped again. Wasn't this still a perfect sunny Sunday? Sue playing piano for the church choir, then a family hike? Things like this didn't happen in St. Louis where Sue had grown up.

Then Sue heard a little moan somewhere close by. She pivoted and ran blindly up the stream bank, scrambling over cacti and boulders. She nearly stumbled over the cougar. It stared at her, Laura hanging from its jaws by her neck. The child's bloody head flopped forward like a rag doll's. Blood ran down her arms and onto the ground.

Sue screamed again, this time making words: "Help! Somebody help me!"

The cougar never blinked.

A man appeared from somewhere, told her to wait while he got a gun, then also disappeared.

Next a slim, dark-skinned man appeared. But he did not disappear. Instead he cracked a limb off a manzanita bush and started shouting at the cougar. He waved the limb and stabbed at its eyes. The cougar batted at the sharp stick. A confused moment later, the man was barking at Sue: "Grab your baby and run!"

She snapped to. The man now stood between the cat and Laura, who had been dropped in a motionless heap. Sue gathered the child up and spun away, her daughter's mangled head cradled against her shoulder.

She nearly collided with her husband. He draped his jacket over Laura and they began to run.

David had found a ranger, who met them in a jeep somewhere near the trailhead. "Don't worry, she'll be OK," the ranger said as he propped Laura up in the seat.

"No," Sue thought. "Don't tell me that. She's going to die."

Sue was wrong: Laura made it. But when she left the hospital five weeks later, Laura had no control over her right side. She couldn't walk. A steel plate patched a hole in her skull. She wore a bike helmet to protect the knitting bones as she stumbled around the house trying to make her body obey the simplest commands.

Orange County closed the park. Two days later, a male lion was shot four hundred yards from the attack site. The county's board of supervisors had a tough choice to make. How long should the closure last? Would this kind of lightning strike again? Biologists said not likely, but had to admit you couldn't be certain unless you killed every cat in the region. Tougher yet, nobody could tell the board for sure that the cat that had been shot was Laura's attacker. An expert tracker reported that the dead lion's tracks, in his opinion, matched tracks from the attack site, but no physical evidence was found when the cat was necropsied.

The closure was not popular. About a month after the attack the park reopened, with extra cougar warning signs in place.

Caspers Wilderness Park is not very wild. White people drove the Juaneño Indians out of the foothills two hundred years ago so they could raise cattle there. Later, a 7,600-acre ranch remnant along San Juan Creek was set aside as Caspers Park. Now San Juan Capistrano and neighboring cities are steadily surrounding it as they move up the canyons toward the Santa Ana Mountains. But just like other foothills parks in the Santa Anas, the dry scrublands and canyon oak forests are full of deer. That makes them wild enough for cougars.

Seven months after the attack, the Smalls sued Orange County and the California Department of Fish and Game. They argued officials had been negligent in failing to warn park visitors that between September of 1985 and March of 1986 there had been seven daytime sightings of unusually bold cougars, about one a month. Three weeks before the attack on Laura, a woman had been stalked by a lion that would not leave until she pelted it with rocks.

And then less than two weeks after the Smalls filed suit, lightning struck again in Caspers Park.

Tim Mellon carried his dream of a backwoods life in the sheath knife he wore at his hip. Paved and populous Southern California was just a place to make good money working construction until the family could move to the mountains. He and his brother-in-law Bill scouted flea markets, collecting ever bigger knives to match their ever bigger dreams.

On October 19, Tim and Bill with both their families and Tim's stepbrother James, drove up the Ortega Highway to Caspers Park. They left their vehicles at a dusty trailhead. Hiking up the oak-canopied trail, Tim thought the park looked like the kind of woodsy countryside where he hoped one day to live.

The pack of children led the adults, all except Tim's son Justin who had stopped to tie his sneakers. The tow-headed six-year-old was just learning his knot so it often came undone. The other adults passed by, but Tim paused while Justin finished. Then he watched the boy run around a curve to catch the other kids.

Not long afterwards, as the adults neared a hairpin turn, Tim heard screaming and the sound of running feet. Justin's sister Aimee appeared first: pale, keening, and running all-out for the car. The other kids were close behind. Justin was not.

Tim's first thought was that some pervert had grabbed the boy. He'd read about bodies ditched along the Ortega Highway from time to time. He ran for his child. As Tim rounded the bend, he saw James frozen in place, staring at something obscured by trailside brush. A few more steps and Tim saw the cougar. It straddled Justin, its hind legs on either side of his head. It bit at Justin's legs. The boy, pinned on his back, kicked fiercely back.

Tim couldn't make himself move: He was no match for this cat. It was huge, all muscles, teeth, and thick fur. It toyed with Justin as though the child was a little rabbit.

Just as the boy seemed about to scrabble free, the cougar bit him again. For Tim, that did it. Scared as he was, he yanked his knife from its sheath and moved in. The cougar grabbed Justin's head in its teeth and began dragging him farther into the thick brush. Tim raised his shaking hand to stab at the cat, but before he could, it had released the boy and moved a few feet away.

Tim picked Justin up and handed him to his wife, Anne, who had run up behind them. The cat's eyes followed the child as though hypnotized. Bill appeared and pushed in front of Anne to stand shoulder-to-shoulder with Tim. The men raised their arms, screaming, "Get the hell out of here!"

The cougar stared a moment longer, then slowly turned and walked into the bushes.

When Justin was rolled into Tim's arms, the boy opened his eyes and looked up at his father.

"Dad, am I going to live?"

Justin was covered with blood. His surfer shorts and T-shirt were in shreds. His bare legs looked like hamburger. So did his head. No way he'd make it, Tim thought.

"Justin, you're going to live," he said.

At the Mission Viejo Trauma Center, surgeons pieced Justin together with more than five hundred stitches. In the waiting room, Tim tried to piece together the kids' story. As they hiked the children had entertained themselves with jokes about the park's poison oak warning and the notes on the map about rattlesnakes and cougars. Justin had just pelted up to the kid group and was down on one knee tying his shoes yet again when he heard another kid yell, "Mountain lion!" He thought it was a psych-out, but then something hit him so hard it knocked him out of his sneakers.

Before they left the hospital, a man approached Tim and introduced himself as a private investigator working for a lawyer up north. Did the family want representation? When the lawyer told Tim about the park's history of cougar incidents, Tim was furious. This was just like that movie *Jaws*, he thought, in which the government lied about danger to protect the tourist trade. By that night, the attorney representing Laura Small had signed up the Mellons, too.

When the Mellons sued, the lawyers used as support a picture taken at Caspers Wilderness Park the day before the attack. A mother is hurrying out of the frame, clutching her child. The toddler is looking over her mother's shoulder at a well-camouflaged cougar. Richard Staskus, the families' lawyer, argued that the county and state had failed to protect park visitors. In addition, he said, Orange County had encouraged rapid development in the foothills without regard for possible impacts on cougar habitat and behavior.

Orange County's board of supervisors closed the park again. What else could they do? Biologists were assuring them the attacks were bad luck, pure and simple. Cougar attacks were incredibly rare. Poison oak really *was* the most dangerous nuisance in the park in terms of the number of people likely to be impacted.

But lawyers for the county warned that if another child were attacked, Orange County would be slaughtered in court, no matter what a hundred biologists said.

The park cautiously reopened three months after Justin's attack. But it was no longer the same place. Children were restricted to picnic areas in the paved-road section. Families with children were not allowed to camp overnight. Cougar warning signs were installed at trailheads and parking lots, and rangers posted hand-written reports after each sighting. Visitors were required to sign liability waivers.

When Laura's case went to trial, jurors were shown a videotape of a happy child dashing after a pet bunny. The tape of Laura after the attack captured a frustrated, disfigured five-year-old fumbling with blocks and crashing about in her helmet. Jurors heard about cougar sightings and confrontations leading up to the attack, looked over park handouts with the jocular warning about poison oak, and awarded the Smalls $2.1 million.

The county's lawyer had argued wild animals were unpredictable and the county couldn't be expected to protect everyone from every possible risk. The jury disagreed. People expected the government to protect them in a county park. The county gave up and quietly settled with the Mellons for about $100,000.

Caspers remained mostly off-limits to kids for more than a decade.

Meanwhile, Justin grew up to be a football star. He read everything he could find about cougars. He figured he got attacked because he was just in the wrong place at the wrong time. Laura learned to walk again and hiked in Caspers and other Santa Ana foothills parks. Although blind in one eye, she became a painter who sometimes produced polemical canvases in favor of wildlife preservation. People had overstepped their bounds, she thought, pushing too far into the cougars' turf. That was why she had been attacked.

Justin and Laura's attitudes were common in California, a state that even after these and other attacks repeatedly upheld the strongest cougar protections in the country.

Orange County reopened Caspers Park to kids on December 16, 1997. Less than two weeks later, two women hiking in the park with young children were rushed by a cougar. Nobody was injured.

"We have to decide if this is a park for children to play in or a park for mountain lions. The two are not compatible," protested County Supervisor Charles Smith. But the county wasn't prepared to make another unpopular decision. They had been heavily criticized for the long closure, and there was no way the public would tolerate cougar extermination. They'd cross their fingers, hope for the best.

The cougar was shot. The park remains open to children. There have been no more attacks.

9

THE SANTA ANA COUGARS

The attacks on Laura Small and Justin Mellon precipitated one of the most in-depth cougar studies in California history. Suddenly everyone wanted to know what was going on with Santa Ana's mountain lions.

Over the next five years researcher Paul Beier and his colleagues followed an eventual total of thirty-two radio-collared cats. What they uncovered surprised almost everyone. The study was partly designed to evaluate human risk, but what it showed most clearly was that, even in a state that allowed no recreational cougar hunting, humans were far more lethal to cougars than *vice versa*. In fact the Santa Ana cougars were dying out.

The Santa Anas are the north end of a series of coastal ranges that run from near Disneyland in Orange County to the Mexican border 135 miles south. From the freeways you can see steep, brushy peaks riven by oak-filled canyons. Saddleback, the Santa Anas' highest point, is dramatic at 5,687 feet but not high enough to capture and hold water-storing snowfields, so most streams on the west slopes run only sporadically. If you stand in the dry gully of one of these foothills canyons, surrounded by chaparral grass, sagebrush, and manzanita, it still feels wild, the kind of place cougars belong.

But there's probably a dirt road snaking past you, and a subdivision on the ridgeline that was not there last year. And faintly in the distance, the sound of bulldozers.

Were the Santa Anas wild enough for cougars? And as they became ever less wild, could the cougar adapt?

One morning a tracker followed a cougar to her grassy daybed in a small canyon northeast of Laura Small's hometown, El Toro. Bulldozers growled into view, carving a new road. The street sign was already in place: ANTONIO PARKWAY, it said. To the north the tracker could see golfers on the new Rancho Margarita. From across the canyon came the gunfire din of hammers building a hundred new homes in Mission Viejo. A half mile south, heavy equipment roared, gouging out the foundations of a new canyon bridge and another road into the Santa Anas. As though oblivious, the cougar rested.

Grad student Dave Choate spent a June evening following a young male cougar who eventually rested near a well-used jogging and biking trail. Two people climbed a ridge above the cat to watch the Disneyland fireworks show in nearby Anaheim. After the show they walked home, passing within about two hundred yards of the bedded cougar.

The Santa Ana cougars were so discreet few people even noticed them. Why couldn't the two species coexist indefinitely?

The eighth male collared in Beier's study was nineteen months old when his mother abandoned him in a dry canyon. Every cougar lucky enough to achieve young adulthood must pass the test he now faced. He lacked the strength, bulk, and skill that would be his in maturity, yet he needed to hunt successfully and learn how to navigate a dangerous world alone.

Midway through his second week alone, the young male made his first large kill, a mule deer fawn. He fed on it for three nights. It was an auspicious start.

He soon found a temporary home range at Trestles Beach, just down the coast from San Clemente. With its rocky beach and empty bluffs, Trestles offers humans world-famous waves and a lonely vibe. There is no road access to the beach. Surfers have to hike in from Interstate 5. What Trestles offered the young cougar was a thick willow forest at the mouth of a creek where he could sleep by day. The creek meant plenty of deer to try for and small game to augment a beginner's diet.

Shortly after they parted ways, his mother had been killed by a car on I-5. When he left the surfer hangout, he passed through her now vacant territory doing what young male cougars do, wandering in search of his own. He moved north along the open scrubby ridges above San Juan Capistrano, hunting the grasslands around the city dump, walking through a commercial nursery and then resting near the city sewage plant.

Most of the time he moved through marginal cougar habitat. But marginal habitat is safest for a young male, especially in regions where good habitat is limited. The punishment for infringing on a big adult male's territory can be death.

Eventually he climbed into the Santa Anas via a mostly dry creek bed on the city limits of Mission Viejo. Over the years Beier's team would track several cats up the same canyon. In places, houses are built right to the steep banks of the brushy little ravine. Where there weren't homes, there were often bulldozers carving out new foundations. For now, however, the ravine was still a corridor to better habitat in the Chino Hills.

At first he stayed in the ravine. Days, he lay in thick brush near trails used by hikers, joggers, and dirt bikers. He never showed himself, never bothered anyone that Beier heard of. Finally, he began to move again— north up the canyon and out of the Santa Anas, then across a freeway into the Chino Hills where a state park and some private ground remained undeveloped. Since the study team hoped to document and encourage the crossbreeding of cougars in the Santa Anas and the Chino Hills, this movement looked like success.

But shortly after arriving in the Chino Hills, the Trestle Beach cougar's collar stopped transmitting. A month later a stalled motorist stumbled on his carcass in a weedy ditch in Pomona. A city of more than 150,000, Pomona is surrounded by other Los Angeles suburbs: Ontario, San Bernardino, Riverside, and Santa Ana. The young male had to have crossed several subdivisions and many roads to reach the spot where an auto killed him, thirty miles from the crest of the Santa Ana Range and far from the last open ground in the foothills.

Beier and his crew collared another young male cougar treed by neighborhood dogs in Temecula, on the east side of the Santa Anas. The young male had been abandoned by his mother and struck out on his own in August of 1990. Soon after collaring, he wound up low in the foothills in a busy little canyon park just east of Santa Ana, a city of more than 300,000.

The canyon winds through a thickly settled neighborhood, but he had chosen well. It was full of deer and smaller prey, and he was successful enough to gain fifteen pounds. He spent his days resting in the densest part of the willow forest, seldom out of earshot of the park's human visitors.

When he moved on he climbed back toward the crest of the Santa Anas toward more open, less developed country. But his luck had run out. As he crossed a newer commuter shortcut called Santiago Canyon Road, he was struck by a car. The collision broke both hind legs.

The young cougar dragged his useless legs a quarter mile into the shelter of a wooded canyon. There was a small spring there, but for the first week he was too weak to crawl to it for a drink. About two weeks after the accident Beier's trackers found an opossum carcass, probably the injured animal's first meal.

Another week passed. The cougar was able to walk again. He limped south out of his tiny hiding spot, managing to travel two miles to a small reservoir adjacent to a subdivision. There he found a willow forest to hide in and plentiful small game. For about three weeks the cougar lived a few dozen yards from subdivision homes, dogs, and people. There were only two reported sightings.

The cougar limped short distances each night, sticking to easy, level terrain. Beier's team continued to find only occasional opossum carcasses, a bad sign since small game barely begins to address the meat requirements of a cougar, much less provide the extra nutrition it would take to heal this one's damaged body.

About five months after the car hit him the young male moved again, finally making his way back to the little canyon park where he had lived so well in those auspicious first weeks after his mother left.

There he lay down in the willow thicket and died.

The rest of the story had written itself on the animal's body. He weighed eighty-two pounds, perhaps half of what he could have. The car collision had broken his right thighbone just above the knee. Massive scar tissue had essentially rebuilt the leg. But although it was usable, it was now turned backward a quarter turn and canted out 20 degrees.

The animal's left thighbone had been broken off at the ball, leaving him without a solid connection between his leg and body. It had not repaired itself in any way. For months the young cougar had hunted and traveled, awaiting the slow approach of death, those two broken ends grinding against each other.

Each year in this unhunted cougar population, more than half of the kittens and a quarter of the adults died. The study found that one in five kittens lived to adulthood. Autos were a leading cause of these deaths. In all, twelve radio-collared cougars and seven uncollared cougars were hit by cars between 1988 and 1992. Young adults searching for a home range were most at risk. It seemed roads and highways were one thing the Santa Ana cats could not adapt to.

Meanwhile, the human residents of Orange County could easily have thought there were more cougars than ever. Cougars were showing up in backyards, city parks, and school-bus stops. One young disperser, the eleventh male collared by the research team, even made it into downtown Oceanside, a city of 128,000. After being abandoned by his mother near San Juan Capistrano, he had headed south into undeveloped land on Camp Pendleton. There he was hit by a car in early 1992. Beier's trackers found a blood splatter on the road, but it must have been a minor injury because the radio-collar signal told them he rested for just two days before moving on down the coast to the San Luis Rey River.

The river corridor is a thin thread of green brush with houses sporadically clustered along it. Deer and other species use it without creating undue ripples among their human neighbors, but it drives straight into the heart of Oceanside. So the young cougar made a fatal error the night he walked downstream, passed under the I-5 bridge, and followed the river deep into the sleeping city.

Just before 3:00 A.M. on February 29, Oceanside Police Sgt. Rick Anthony was flagged down by a man who said he'd just seen a cougar on the beach. Dispatch was reporting other sightings. When Anthony spotted the animal, it was dashing through the grounds of an apartment building and up a staircase onto a nearby road bank. Anthony called in the sighting. The decision was quickly made that the cougar should be captured and removed.

State animal-control officers, more accustomed to catching unlicensed dogs, succeeded only in frightening the cougar off the road bank. It escaped into another apartment complex. By then, there were eight police officers, three animal-control officers, and an apartment security guard on the chase. They surrounded the apartment building. While the animal control officers searched the interior, a security guard called to say the cat was on the roof. The police officers on the ground spotted it jumping from balconies to rooftops, northbound.

By now the city was waking up. Anthony and his colleagues decided capture was not possible. It was time to shoot the cat before somebody got hurt.

When the cougar was located again, apparently attempting to be invisible, Anthony lined up four officers and directed them to shoot with him on the count of three. At the staccato cracks the cat bolted. In his path was a Fish and Game officer. The man fired. The cat spun away and again tried to flee. The officers followed blood spots up the street.

A few blocks away, they found the cougar holed up under a porch. Sergeant Anthony, twenty feet away and on the far side of a five-foot fence, aimed at its head and fired. The cat ran straight at him. Anthony fired nine more shots. The cougar fell at the other side of the fence. The Fish and Game officer fired one final round behind the cat's ear.

There is no mention in Anthony's report of the one-pound radio collar the animal wore, nor of any attempt to call Beier's research team, who were known to be working with cougars in the area and who had experience in capturing cougars.

Consider the odds against replacing this one young cat. For starters, two females would have to become pregnant, something not to be taken for granted since the team had seen years in which fertile females went unbred in the Santa Anas. Then this hypothetical pair of females would have to beat the one-in-four odds against annual adult survival in this population and give birth to five kittens between them. Four would die in the first year. While the possible replacement cougar was growing to young adulthood, his future chance at viable territory would shrink with every new homesite notched into the foothills of the Santa Anas.

Despite the adaptability and resilience of individual cats, the Santa

Ana cougar population as a whole was made fragile by their rapidly shrinking habitat. During the study's final years, the six counties of Southern California contained 5 percent of the people in the United States. The cities bordering the northern Santa Anas were on pace to double in fifteen years to about 2.3 million people. The 8.8 million people of Los Angeles were spreading south toward the growing suburbs of San Diego, population 2.5 million.

It takes a certain minimum number of adult cougars to maintain any population. In the Santa Anas, Beier calculated that minimum was two dozen. Two dozen adults and the youngsters in their orbits would need some 1,400 square miles of open land. In 1993 the undeveloped lands in the Santa Anas totaled just 1,287 square miles. About half was protected from development.

Beier thought the cats might yet survive if people were willing to preserve narrow corridors of undeveloped ground connecting to bigger patches just outside the Santa Anas, like beads on a string. Could such a necklace substitute for a single large tract of habitat?

More recent research has fine-tuned our understanding of cougar population dynamics. Cougars live, say researchers, either in source or sink populations. A source population produces "excess" animals. The Santa Ana cougars are a sink population. Source populations are stabilized by exporting their young adults, particularly males. Sink populations are stabilized by importing them.

After the study concluded, and in order to preserve the Santa Ana cougars, conservation groups began buying up tracts of ground to act as the wildlife corridors Beier and others had envisioned. But success would have meant cooperation between seventeen California cities and five counties, all competing for new housing and jobs and spur growth. Sources and sinks do not factor heavily into planning and zoning meetings.

By late 1999 there was little support for the extraordinary efforts that might ensure cougar survival in the Santa Anas. Steve Torres, the biologist in charge of California's cougar program, took the weary tone of a doctor waiting for a family to unplug a loved one on life support. Only through artificial means such as transplantation would the Santa Anas continue to be home to cougars in the long term, Torres said.

There was not enough land. There were too many roads.

And then the TCA (Transportation Corridor Agencies) proposed a sixteen-mile, four-lane segment of toll road that would bite into some of the area's biggest remaining chunks of protected land. The TCA promises the artery will cut rush hour commuter time from Oso Parkway to the county line from an hour down to twenty-five minutes. Construction is slated to begin in 2008. The new artery will cost between $500 million and $1.1 billion.

Paul Beier has said he believes land west of the new artery will become unusable to cougars. More important, where roads go development follows. The TCA itself seemed to shrug resignedly at the likely impacts, saying, "Habitat fragmentation primarily due to urbanization is irreversible."

And that, wrote an angry local reporter named Scott Giffin in 2004, "is a good thing if your goal is to eradicate *Puma concolor*."

10

THE URBAN COUGAR

The radio in Ray Kahler's truck crackled: "P.D. reports a young moose sighted at Ferris, last seen headed east."

Ray wheeled his truck around, keying his mike to tell the dispatcher he was on his way. He was a Washington Department of Fish and Wildlife game warden, and sometimes hunting was his job. But Ray wasn't head-quartered in mountainous backcountry. This summer morning in 1999 he would hunt moose in midday traffic in Spokane, a city of four hundred thousand. Ferris, where the moose had sought refuge, was one of the biggest high schools in town.

Wild animals came into town all the time, especially in summer when the surrounding hills got dry. Once Ray got a call from a suburb north of Spokane. A man wanted a moose removed from his swimming pool. It turned out the moose had been enjoying midday dips all summer. The man was calling only because his grandkids had come to visit and wanted to go swimming.

Ray idled his truck along vacant lots between Ferris and a gated sub-division, peering into bushes and pasture grass. Nothing. He radioed back to report no luck. This moose would probably escape town without inci-dent. Most did. But moose are only the most common of Spokane's unwelcome visitors. A bear once foraged its way up the banks of the Spokane River to downtown Riverside Park. Ray captured it a few blocks from the upscale boutiques that face the Opera House. He once hunted a cougar in the asphalt canyons between St. Luke's, Sacred Heart, Deaconess, and Shriners Hospitals. Callers had said it was killing cats and dogs. Ray scoured the area every time a call came in but never caught a glimpse. And one day the calls simply stopped.

In nearly every western city there's a Ray Kahler, a warden who has learned to track big game down city streets. While urban backyards, greenbelts, and parks aren't great wildlife habitat, they'll sometimes do, especially when those backyards were once wildlands.

The idea of conservation, of tempering resource exploitation with an eye to sustainability, was born in this country in the late 1800s. For many species, it came barely in time. By 1890, for example, it was estimated that only 300,000 whitetail deer remained in the entire country. *Branta canadensis maxima*, the western subspecies of migratory Canada geese, hung on by a wingtip.

Two assumptions distinguished the revolutionary new paradigm: a premise that wildlife was vulnerable, scarce, and therefore precious, and a belief that the human and "natural" worlds were separate. Industrial-scale slaughter of species like deer was replaced by controlled recreational hunting and a no-waste, fair chase ethic. Deer were reintroduced into areas from which they'd been eradicated. Parklands were set aside. In the east, where little public land remained, the government purchased ground. At first, predators were killed in even greater numbers because it was believed they would impede deer and elk recovery. But by the early 1960s even predators were viewed more kindly.

For many species, conservation succeeded. Somewhere between fifteen and twenty-five million deer inhabit this country today. Canada geese now number four million, although along the way some populations lost the desire to migrate. Disgusted home owners call them lawn carp. Several predators recovered as well, particularly coyotes, black bears, alligators, and cougars.

In recent decades, certain species have begun to claim human landscapes as their own. Their own recoveries have coincided with rapid suburbanization. Census data shows more Americans move to suburbs than cities. And new suburban neighborhoods gobble land fast, which is why Seattle's acreage grew more than twice as fast as its population from 1970 to 1990, and Los Angeles sprawls six times faster than it adds people.

Humans are the dominant fact for every species among us. We are the weather. For some—perhaps the grizzly bear, the wolverine, and the Snake River salmon—we're the next ice age, an event they are not equipped to survive. But other species thrive among us, at least for now. Humanscapes are potential homes for any species that can adapt to us. If it weren't for his carnivory, the cougar would be among the best candidates for city life: A moose in downtown Spokane immediately causes a commotion. The cryptic, solitary, night-wandering cougar does not. And not creating commotion is the first key to coexisting with humans.

But occasionally a hundred-plus-pound predator in the middle of a city is going to attract attention, particularly if he ends up in the wrong place or is one of those rare cougars who don't mind being seen. Bill Hillis has been a park ranger since 1993, a job which gives him a far better than average chance at seeing wildlife. Yet his best cougar sighting occurred in Chula Vista, a suburb of San Diego. Ground had been broken for a new housing development, so one Sunday afternoon he, his wife, and, two-year-old daughter went hunting fossils among the freshly turned dirt.

Bill recalls a stranger saying to him, "Hey, is that a dog?"

He glanced up to see a large animal sauntering across a newly land-scaped berm bordering a row of backyards. "I think so."

"You sure?" said the man. "Looks like a mountain lion to me."

Bill really looked this time—and realized the man was right. He and his wife watched for perhaps five minutes before the big cat sauntered out of sight, perhaps heading toward one of the wooded canyons which reach down from forested ridges into the suburb.

In Boulder, Colorado, in the mid-1980s, researchers Jim Halfpenny and Michael Sanders asked citizens to report cougar sightings. The results were surprising. One caller had watched a cougar give birth under a neighbor's porch. Another saw a cougar scale a roof to bat at a weather-vane. One Boulder elementary school's sandbox was found to be serving double duty: playground equipment by day, cougar litter box by night.

Managing our feline neighbors is difficult, wardens say, but managing the human side of the equation is nearly as hard and a lot more tangled.

In Sacramento, wildlife-capture expert Bob Teagle can look out the window of Fish and Game's Region II office onto a riverside greenbelt where he occasionally finds cougar tracks. He believes the prints belong not to transients passing through but to cats whose territories include the American River as it sweeps through town, cats who make part of their living off plentiful city deer. "We believe cougars are utilizing all the available habitat," he says. "Including riparian areas inside cities."

Unlike some wardens who take a dim view of urban cougars, even unobtrusive ones, he's decided that as long as they're not bothering anyone, he's not going to bother them. "It's no different than buying a luxury home on a golf course," he tells suburbanites who report a fleeting sight of a cougar. "You gotta expect a few golf balls in your yard." As long as the cougar is only passing through, Bob tells them, the animal should be left alone.

One morning in March 2006, residents of a Boulder, Colorado, neighborhood reported a cougar moving through their backyards. It confronted nobody, but several who saw it were disturbed enough to call 911. One woman watching the animal cross her backyard described herself as scared and "shaking." Emergency dispatch did not forward the calls to the Colorado Division of Wildlife for four hours, according to CBS. So the callers waited for a response that did not come.

The Division of Wildlife spokesperson responded as Bob Teagle would have, saying, "This cat has not behaved in an aggressive manner and wasn't considered a threat to any area residents." Residents who disagreed were angry. To them, a cougar in their yard was absolutely a threat.

In 1994 the state of Montana responded to increasing predator conflicts around the resort town of Kalispell by creating a new position. About half of Erik Wenum's job as bear and lion wildlife biologist involves what he calls conflict management. Soon after he took the post, he was summoned to a well-tended neighborhood three blocks east of Kalispell's City Hall. A cougar had killed a house cat there and lain down on a manicured lawn to eat it.

"The reason we have large predators on the landscape is because the public allows it," says Erik. And the public allows predators because of the unwritten contract that says that when people express concern, wildlife officers will respond.

But there are responses the public does not want to accept, says Gerry Brunham, the grizzled former Vancouver Island game warden. They don't want to see armed men tramping through their backyards. They don't want to hear hounds tearing through suburban streets on a hot scent trail. And they particularly don't want to hear wardens say that cougars are in our cities to stay until we kill them, starve out the in-town deer, and log off every in-town thicket where a cougar could hide.

Typically, people would insist that he respond to a sighting, but they didn't want him to kill the cat. He once shot a sheep-killing cougar near a popular hiking trail on the edge of Victoria, capital city of the province. Next thing he knew, a woman had written to the *Victoria Times-Colonist* to say, "We pay conservation officers to help save animals, not kill them. I think it's awful that a conservation officer would shoot and kill a cougar that could have easily been tranquilized and moved somewhere else. . . . I think that the conservation officer who shot it for no particular reason should be charged and definitely should not have this job. He should work in a slaughterhouse."

Gerry had been on the job a long time when that letter appeared. It did not surprise him.

"They think it's the last cougar in the world and I murdered it. Sometimes they think I enjoyed it," said Gerry.

Enforcement officer Paul Mosman lacks that long experience, but his education got a jump start not long after his transfer from rural Port Angeles, Washington, to Spokane in 2005. Dispatch had called in with a report of a possible cougar attack on a dog in a ritzy South Hill backyard. Twenty minutes later Paul was at the home. The dog owner was not.

He looked around the yard for tracks or evidence of a struggle. Nothing. And it didn't make sense to call out a houndsman to see what dogs might find. The weather was hot and dry, horrible trailing conditions, and the volunteer houndsmen who help the department were seldom willing to run their valuable animals through backyards and across roads. Besides, it was getting harder to find houndsmen these days: Washington voters had outlawed hound hunting, so there was no longer a legal way for hunters to train their animals.

Paul called the dog owner at work. She told him the incident had occurred the previous night at about 10:00 P.M., when she'd let her nine-pound dog outside. A few minutes later she had heard a commotion and stepped outside. Her dog was on its back and something large and brown was running away.

Paul thought the conversation went well. He asked her to describe the brown shape. She'd only had a glimpse but thought it might have weighed about ninety pounds. He explained that it was possible, based on her limited description, that she'd seen a cougar, but if so he'd found no sign of it. He explained why he wouldn't run hounds and how it was more likely that the animal had been a dog. He offered the usual advice about living with pets in cougar country and went back to patrolling.

He was a little surprised when the woman called back a few hours later. She wanted to know if the department was aware that other South Hill residents had been seeing a black cougar. She wanted to know if that might have been what jumped her dog.

Paul told her what he knew: Black variants of many species exist. It's a color phase, however, that's never been documented in mountain lions. It was possible, based on her description, that she had seen a cougar; more likely she had not.

Paul was off work for three days. When he returned, it was to a small typhoon. Every media outlet in the city had been calling the department. So had many citizens. Paul's sergeant wanted to know what the hell Paul was thinking, telling a citizen that a cougar had attacked her dog. He asked why Paul had estimated this hypothetical animal's size, based on tracks he told the citizen he'd found, at 130 pounds; and why he'd said it was possible that a black panther was "on the loose" in the South Hill area. None of those things had been mentioned in Paul's report three days before.

In the newspaper stories Paul read, the woman had not simply seen a brown shape running away. She had seen it holding her dog in its mouth.

Paul's storm blew over in a few weeks, although he is still sometimes asked about the black panther on South Hill. He no longer assumes that nervous people understand what he's saying just because they nod and say yes. He is quick to point out that he doesn't think the woman lied. He thinks she believed every word she said. Luckily for Paul, his sergeant believed him.

Ray Kahler's lesson was to be more painful. His bad day started one morning in 1998 as he was gathering gear for a well-earned day of turkey hunting in the mountains north of Spokane. Across town, South Hill residents had spotted a cougar near Manito Park. A dozen police cars had been directed to scour the neighborhood. Then dispatch called Ray, herder of parking-lot moose, trapper of downtown bears.

Swinging down from his truck at the impromptu police command post, Ray stepped into a circus. Patrolmen's radios chattered with reports, dispatchers relayed orders, and officers in cruisers hustled pedestrians off the sidewalks. Two sniper teams were standing by in full regalia. The only performer missing was the cougar. Police hadn't located him.

Ray shook his head. If they just waited, the animal would probably go to sleep in a quiet spot and then, in darkness, sneak away.

He was relieved when it became apparent that the police were running out of patience. He quickly agreed that their patrol cars could be put to better use in downtown traffic. The search would be continued by a team of police volunteers.

Ray headed home to grab his turkey gear.

His phone rang again a little after 9:00 A.M. The cougar had lost its chance to slip out of town. It had been chased into a tree near the corner of Tekoa and 26th. This time, expecting an even larger crowd and some attention from his superiors at Fish and Game, Ray put on his uniform.

He knew he only had two choices: Shoot the cat on the spot or dart and relocate it. Ray believed that a cougar willing to wander deep into a city and get caught there needed to be removed from the population. He may have been drawn by hunger coupled with attractants like backyard pets or tame, garden-browsing deer. Perhaps all the good habitat was occupied by other cougars. Either way, darting the animal and carting him out to a clearing did not eliminate the underlying cause of his presence in town. Besides, as Ray well knew, there's nothing humane about relocation.

Recently some states have begun taking a similar hard line, telling the public that cougars which can't be left in place will be killed rather than relocated. This approach relieves some callers and offends others. If Erik Wenum is faced with a choice between removing a cougar and killing it, he will kill it. He may dart and transport it discreetly out of sight first, but not always. "Sometimes you don't want to give people an out. . . . I may be the guy with the unpleasant job of shooting the lion, but I did not cause its death. The people who fed the deer or the turkeys in their backyard are far more responsible than I am," says Erik.

But in 1998 official policy hadn't yet caught up with uncomfortable reality. Arriving at the scene, Ray saw policemen trying to hold back a crowd of a hundred people. All three local TV stations were on hand, cameras running. Three snipers, two in full SWAT gear, were stationed at the base of a ponderosa pine. Forty-five feet above them all, a big tom cougar stared down at the ruckus.

Police told him their orders were to shoot the cat if it came out of the tree. Ray looked at the crowd, the rows of homes marching down 26th, curious faces in some of the windows. A bullet would be a far more dangerous item here than a cougar.

Across the street one of the TV crews was engaged in a shoving match with a couple of cops. It looked like the reporters were being arrested. Ray meanwhile could do little until the veterinarian arrived with tranquilizers. He didn't like the animal's tense, twitchy posture. This was turning into what cops call "a situation."

When the vet finally arrived, Ray had been envisioning worst case scenarios for more than an hour. The animal leaping down and bowling into a child; police spraying bullets after a scampering cat; the anesthetic, never completely reliable, putting a confused cougar on the ground in the middle of a hundred people. He needed a safe outcome the public could stomach. The cougar should die—it was the kindest thing and the right thing—but it couldn't be shot from that tree in front of this crowd.

"I want you to O.D. this cat," Ray said quietly to the vet.

The vet didn't argue. He loaded what Ray assumed was a lethal dose in his tranquilizer gun. But his first shot missed. The cat started at the ping of the dart hitting a nearby branch, and climbed higher. Hurrying now, the vet loaded a second hypo, stepped forward, sighted, and shot. A clean hit. The cat crept out to the weak end of its limb. As the branch dipped, the cat slipped and toppled more than thirty feet to the ground. Ray didn't let out his breath until it settled back onto its haunches, convulsed, and lay still.

"Good job," a voice called from the crowd. Considering how wrong it could have gone, Ray thought so too.

Other voices asked how long the cougar would be unconscious, whether it was all right, where it would be taken. Ray told them what he believed they wanted to hear. The animal was fine. When it recovered, it would be returned to the wilderness and freed.

Then Ray Kahler drove back to the Fish and Wildlife office on Division Street, expecting the cat to be dead by the time he arrived. Instead it was bouncing off the walls of the box.

Ray told his boss the whole story. If he expected to be commended for defusing a touchy situation, he was disappointed. Mike Whorton was unhappy that Ray had opted to kill the cat, unhappier still that he had lied. One of the agency's rules back then was that cougars had to pose a threat before they could be killed. The cat had been up a tree. What harm could it have done there? Ray found himself trying to argue his boss into his shoes earlier that day. Too many police with guns drawn; too many onlookers; an unpredictable, frightened animal with sharp claws and teeth. In that situation the cat did not have to *mean* harm to cause it.

They moved on to the next sticky question: What now?

Ray wanted to finish what he'd started. "What would be more humane?" he asked. "Giving it a shot there in the back of the truck or releasing it to die in the woods?"

But management didn't care. Ray had promised people the cat would be released. He had to keep the promise.

At the drop site, Ray and a colleague spilled the cat from its cage. He watched it walk to a log, shakily the way a drugged animal does. Then it sank down to rest. It was still lying there when he drove away. Ray began to think that, despite the drugs and its hard fall, it might survive.

A few hours later, uncertain why it suddenly mattered, he returned to check on the animal. The cat was lying dead near where he'd last seen it. He told his boss.

"Agent Lied–They Meant to Kill Cougar" shouted the page one headline a week and a half later. Somehow, the newspaper had found out.

Bruce Smith, the Spokane Region Director of Washington Fish and Wildlife, issued a public apology. His statement didn't offer even token support for his veteran sergeant. Smith announced an investigation into whether Ray should be fired. A letter of reprimand went into his file.

Newspaper articles and letters to the editor made Ray into a villain. They stung so badly that Ray took time off work. Tina Bjorklund, in whose yard the cougar had treed, hung a sign, THE PUMA PONDEROSA and told *Spokesman-Review* reporter Adam Lynn, "I don't like the people I pay taxes to lying to me like that."

Ray Kahler's storm never completely died out. He retired in 2001, the thunder and lightning still fresh in his mind. He hears from friends on the job that things have gotten better, and wonders if his ordeal helped spur the change. He knows that colleagues wrote to the state commissioners in support of his actions that day.

Washington now has a new "no tolerance" policy for problem and urban cougars. It gives enforcement officers the decision-making latitude Ray needed that day.

But the most awkward part of the equation remains, say game wardens. Their bosses may have changed their tunes but the public has not: It's fine if public funds and agency time are spent on the issue, but only so long as wardens remove the problem without killing anything. Until that public mandate becomes more realistic, guys like Ray have a hard, hard job.

Since cougars are elusive, shy, and primarily nocturnal, the best opportunity to see one in the wild is usually after it has been treed by hounds. Mark Miller photographed this cat (above, and on the next page, inset) near Corwin Springs, Montana, after a friend with dogs called to say he had found a set of very fresh tracks.

Photographer Mark Miller had heard rumors of mountain lions in an area north of Yellowstone National Park. Taking a walk above Bear Creek roughly two miles from Jardine, Montana, he spotted a mountain lion female down in the creek bed, her three kittens playing around her. He stood unnoticed, watching them play. After leaving for lunch, when he returned he was spotted immediately, the mother's stare finding him from a distance of several hundred yards.

*Several years ago, Jim Heustess was photographing
whitetail deer on Montana's National Bison Range.
Through his viewfinder, he watched as the deer tensed,
fixed on a point over his shoulder, and then fled, tails
flashing. A mother cougar with three kittens emerged
out of the draw behind him. The first kitten into the
field turned to look at the camera, and Heustess's
shutter clicked. In a flash it was gone.*

Jim Mepham photographed this rare cougar attack sequence in 1992 at Glacier National Park's Walton Goat Lick.

After being captivated by the sight of a cougar stalking and killing a mountain goat, Mepham had the disconcerting experience of feeling the predator's eye turn on him. No longer observer but participant, Mepham quickly retreated, leaving the cougar to his meal.

Jim Mepham

Within the growing community of professional wildlife photographers, there is a rift between those who include captive animals in their portfolios and those who restrict themselves to shooting images of only wild animals. When this family of mountain lions began appearing outside their den on the National Elk Refuge near Jackson, Wyoming, they attracted the attention of a number of photographers from around the world, including local photographer Bruce Becker.

Bruce Becker, Teton Photo Works

11

THE EASTERN COUGAR

Unlike the sheer peaks of the Rockies, the mountains of Virginia's Shenandoah National Park are forested to their summits. Their gray spines, worn as the molars of an old grizzly, erupt and crumble back into dense vegetation.

The forests appear ageless and enduring, but this is not the landscape that met the first immigrants to Appalachia. As elsewhere in the East, those original forests were razed. The species which inhabited them were decimated.

Cougars once spanned the continent, living in every ecosystem that provided sufficient numbers of a large ungulate, preferably deer, and cover from which to hunt them. This included the vast majority of the East. It is generally—and incorrectly—accepted that human guns, traps, and poisons eradicated cougars east of Colorado by the end of the nineteenth century.

The fact is that despite best efforts, we are not directly responsible for the demise of the eastern cougar. Cougars survived hundreds of years of predator bounties coupled with humanity's reflexive distaste only to sink from sight when their primary prey, the deer, were essentially wiped out.

Almost as soon as deer numbers began to rebound, easterners began again to report cougar sightings. Then in 1972 a population of thirty to fifty tragically inbred animals was discovered in the Florida Everglades. Despite all this, the official position of eastern wildlife agencies has for many decades been that eastern cougar sightings are erroneous, and that outside of Florida, the eastern cougar is gone. In 1973 the U.S. Fish and Wildlife Service implicitly contradicted this stance by listing the eastern subspecies as endangered.

Most eastern cougar sightings probably are erroneous. Bobcats, common in the East, are the same approximate shape. Deer and golden retrievers are the same color. A person glimpses something moving in dense vegetation and his imagination fills in the blanks so rapidly that it is the constructed composite, not the parts actually seen, that becomes memory. Even in the West where cougars are relatively common, researchers say the majority of cat sightings are false. Coyotes, bobcats, deer, and the common house cat have all been frequently misidentified as cougars, in some cases even by wildlife professionals.

In the past decade sighting reports have accelerated across the East but, more interesting, there is now physical proof that cougars exist outside the West. Midwestern cougars have been shot, hit by cars, and even radio collared. As recently as seven years ago, experts "knew" the cougar was found only in twelve western states, British Columbia, and part of Texas. But if we plot recent confirmed cougar locations outside those states, we get a line that runs from the tip of Lake Superior to southeastern Louisiana.

Could it be true, as the U.S. Fish and Wildlife Service seemed to think, that the cougar survived in the East, not just in the Everglades but in other tiny pockets as well? Far likelier is that young western cougars, driven to disperse, occasionally travel greater distances than has been assumed normal. It's not unusual for a mountain lion to travel two hundred miles in search of acceptable adult territory. Researchers studying a recently acknowledged population of cougars in South Dakota documented dispersals of six hundred miles or more. Collared South Dakota cougars ended up in Montana, Minnesota, and even Oklahoma.

Other valid eastern cougar sightings are almost certainly what eastern wildlife managers call FERCs, or "Feral Escaped or Released Captive." Cougars breed well in captivity. Cougar kittens, fuzzy and spotted, make adorable pets. It is not hard to obtain a kitten even though in some states it is not legal.

But then the cat begins to grow. He becomes expensive to feed and hard to manage. Some carefully raised captive cougars will purr like house-cats when petted, and lick your hand with a raspy tongue. But no cougar handler turns his back on that animal, not ever. Even declawed it still has teeth. So the cage door is "accidentally" left ajar one night, perhaps by an owner convinced he is doing a kindness for an animal better off free.

In the end it almost doesn't matter whether authentic cougar sightings in the East are surviving natives, FERCs, or dispersing cougars from other regions. The fact is that some few sightings are almost certainly authentic. And that raises far more interesting questions. Will the mostly urban inhabitants of this densely populated region make room for the cougar? And if they don't, is the cougar capable of making a place for himself?

The day the first free-roaming cougar is confirmed in the East will be a tough one for the warden who winds up in the hot seat, for all the usual reasons. What will make it worse is that, in the East, the animal is plagued with an identity crisis.

In the late nineteenth and early twentieth centuries, scientists were engaged in breaking species into subspecies. Subspecies could be distinguished from one another both by geographic separation and by physical dissimilarities that developed over time. It was generally agreed that the cougar was comprised of thirty-two subspecies, twelve in the United States and Canada and the rest in Central and South America. Two of the North American subspecies are currently listed as endangered. One of these, *puma concolor coryii*, is the Florida panther. The other, *puma concolor couguar*, is the eastern cougar.

But a funny thing happened on the way to subspeciation. By the time serious work on cougar subspecies began in the 1940s, nobody had actually captured or killed an eastern cougar in decades. The necessary skeletal measurements and pelt observations were performed on a handful of skulls, skeletons, and hides from museums and private collections. The total number of samples used to describe the eastern cougar? Eight. Six other subspecies were described from one specimen each, say researchers Linda Sweanor and Kenny Logan.

Then along came the twenty-first century and genetic marking as a way of describing subspecies. When researcher Melanie Culver applied these new tools to the cougar, a very different picture emerged. What Culver found in the DNA samples available to her was that all North American cougars were so genetically alike as to be one subspecies. This included the Florida panther and the eastern cougar. South American cougars *are* genetically different from North American cougars, apparently. But all across our continent, the cougar is simply himself: panther, painter, mountain lion—our three-hundred-thousand-year-old native son.

What do game agencies do about an endangered species science now says never existed? What the state of Missouri recently did was change the eastern cougar's designation from "endangered" to "extirpated." The term has a specific meaning for biologists. It refers to a species eliminated through part but not all of its range. Arkansas made a similar move in 2001.

Missouri and Arkansas are responding to three facts. Cougars have been recently documented in both states. Neither state's game managers welcome this news. And the awkward promise of Culver's research is that it will now be impossible to either identify or rule out a wild cougar as an eastern cougar. Since eastern cougars are federally protected, confirmation is as politically necessary as it is scientifically impossible: Western cougars can be killed. Eastern cougars must be actively assisted.

And both states know it's a matter of time before one of their game wardens stands looking at an honest-to-god cougar, a crowd of bystanders at his back, trying to figure whether he's supposed to treat the cornered animal before him as a rare orchid, a strange seedling, or a weed.

12

IN SEARCH OF THE EASTERN COUGAR

In 2004 Barbara Chaplin decided to have a culvert removed from a creek on her property outside of Winchester, Virginia. She lives two hours from Washington, D.C., on forty forested acres.

As she watched the contractors work, she noticed fresh tracks in the mud. Amateur naturalist that she is, she stooped to examine them. They were huge prints from an animal's front and rear foot, plus the right rear knee where the animal had sat on its haunches.

They didn't look like dog tracks, and they were too big for coyote. Anyway there were no canid claw marks. Nor were they bear tracks. She called the workmen over to take a look.

"Cougar," they said after squatting to study the tracks. She did not question this—the men were locals and hunters, and they sounded sure.

Over the next few days Barbara talked about the cougar tracks she'd seen. None of her neighbors appeared surprised, and she continued to think little of it.

Then in February of 2005 she got a phone call from the Michigan Wildlife Conservancy's Dennis Fijalkowski, where her daughter volunteered.

"You found a cougar track on your land?" he asked. "You have to do something about this."

"Why?"

"Don't you know they're supposed to be extirpated?"

She had not known. Around her neighborhood, she told him, every-one knew the opposite.

"Everyone knowing" and proof were not the same thing, Dennis replied.

And Cougar Quest was born.

Barbara calls it "citizen science": people armed with the passion to find an answer and whatever education they can glean from books, pamphlets, and helpful experts. Cougar Quest's goal is to document the existence of cougars in Virginia with solid evidence.

When I visited Barbara, she was very excited about something nested in tissue in what looked to be a takeout salad box. The item appeared to be a hairball, segmented and about the size of my thumb. Barbara was hoping it was cougar scat. As this book goes to press, she still awaits final DNA test results.

The best evidence she's collected besides that twist of hair and bone is a plaster cast of a track. Of the eight experts who evaluated it, six responded that the track cast was either definitely or possibly a cougar's. Two said it definitely was not.

Barbara's is one of several grassroots organizations devoted to proving that cougars inhabit the East. Neighboring West Virginia is home to the Eastern Cougar Foundation. When founder Todd Lester was in high school, he went hunting with his dogs one day and saw what he was positive was a cougar. Like many who report sightings to eastern authorities, he was laughed at. Years later, still certain of what he had seen that day, Todd began his own search for proof, which eventually morphed into the ECF.

"[State biologists] don't have the funding or the staff. They can't follow up on sighting reports. They want proof, but where will the proof come from?" asks Barbara.

In the late 1970s the Forest Service and U.S. Fish and Wildlife Service also tried to obtain proof. They hired wildlife biologist Robert Downing to conduct track surveys.

Many believed he would find the proof. One of the largest chunks of public land in the East lies along the spine of the Appalachians between West Virginia and Virginia. Contained within this habitat is the

Cranberry Wilderness, a 36,000-acre roadless area in the Monongahela National Forest. It's believed that deer never completely died out in the Cranberry. And if there were always deer, is it not possible that there have always been cougars?

On the other hand, the last officially accepted wild cougar kills in Virginia and West Virginia occurred in the 1880s. In 1936 Smithsonian researchers confirmed cougar tracks in Pocahontas County, West Virginia, but none have been confirmed since.

After three years of track surveys, Downing's careful research netted exactly one possible track and one scat suspected to be from a cougar. But Downing had become a believer. He pointed out in his report that tracking conditions are seldom favorable in the dense deciduous forests of the East, so different from the snowier, more open and arid West. He wanted the search to continue.

Of the handful of contemporary scientists who have tried to track the eastern cougar question on the ground, perhaps the most interesting work has been conducted by Jim Atkinson, a biologist at Shenandoah National Park.

Funding to study an animal thought to be extirpated is tough to arrange, but when a seasonal employee came to him in 1997 asking that they try to document cougars in the park, Jim happened to have some remote-triggering cameras lying around from a bear study that had lost funding. He also had a curious nature, a stack of park cougar sightings in his files, and a strong preference for fieldwork over paperwork.

Karen Hathaway, the employee, had been responsible for one of those sighting reports. The previous year she was driving with her daughter along Skyline Drive, the park's famous scenic throughway.

"Look, Mom, a lion!" her daughter had said.

Karen's eyes followed her daughter's pointing finger. Later she would distinctly remember the animal's long tail, swishing back and forth near the ground.

Jim arranged for volunteers and a supply of road-killed deer to use as camera bait. The team mapped the park's cougar sightings to find likely camera locations. Then the study began.

Three years after its conclusion, Jim and I sat in a conference room looking at slides. There were many, many images of bears, lots of bobcats, gray and red foxes, raccoons, skunks, and flying squirrels. And not one single cougar.

Jim believes that if there had been cougars in Shenandoah while his study was active, he would have a picture of one. But he is still unwilling to dismiss all the park's cougar sightings. In 1994 a botanist reported almost hitting a cougar on Skyline Drive. "You could not tell that man he didn't see what he saw," said Jim.

He also takes a lesson from the ivory-billed woodpecker. Supposedly extinct since the 1940s, the distinctively colored bird was sighted and then photographed in Arkansas in 2004.

He finds an even more interesting lesson in the coyote. Unlike cougars and ivory-billed woodpeckers, coyotes never lived in the East. But they do now. They began to be reported in the park starting in the early 1990s. At first people did not believe those sightings either, but now Jim and his team, through this project, have the first park photographs of these wary little predators.

I asked Jim what would have happened had he succeeded in documenting cougars in the park as well.

He laughed. "Our public affairs person would have flipped!"

The day before, I had put the same question to the state nongame biologist in charge of Virginia's cougar issue.

"I'm not certain what we would do with [a free-roaming cougar]," Rick Reynolds had said. "We would try to confirm the evidence, but after that? If you find that one is really out there, what do you do? I suppose we'd go after it. Most likely it would go to a zoo."

Jack Wallace is an endangered species biologist for West Virginia's Department of Natural Resources. When cougar sightings are reported in West Virginia, they usually fall in his lap.

"People around here are unimpressed with the thought of cougars returning. You tell them it's an umbrella species...they don't care. What they care about is that the animal is large and dangerous and kills their deer," says Jack.

Rural, forested West Virginia would probably be as hospitable to cougars as Idaho or Montana. The state boasts one million acres of national forest and about 800,000 whitetail deer. It has fewer than two million people, a number which until recently has been slowly shrinking.

Jack's cougar report file is about an inch thick; it spans half a century with the majority of reports recent. It is a study in how difficult the eastern cougar issue is. For one thing, the data are not processed in any meaningful way. Like his counterparts in other states, Jack has no funding to do more than take calls and write up reports. He knows that many sightings go unreported. People are wary of the agency, its regulations, and its historic response to cougar sightings.

Leafing through the file, I find many of the reports easy to dismiss.

Someone hears a scream in the night and then neighborhood dogs barking wildly. They decide they have been visited by a cougar. Or several sheep are killed and then someone finds a large footprint. Despite the fact that dogs are the likeliest killers of livestock in the East, the caller is sure the track was made by a cougar.

But for each year there are several reports that are hard to dismiss. They include concise, accurate descriptions of mountain lions by people who had a span of time to observe the animal or who were not alone and whose companions also observed the animal. One letter writer emphatically asserted that the state's official position, that the cougar is extirpated in West Virginia, is wrong-headed, the result of scientists being unwilling to accept one kind of data (sightings) while simultaneously begging for another kind (tracks, scats, or carcasses).

It is hard to believe that every one of those reports could be explained away if you were privy to all the facts. It makes far more sense that West Virginia hosts a few cougars, now and then, here and there, whether survivors, FERCs, or immigrants.

There have certainly been two. No matter your position on the desirability of cougar recovery in the East, the story as told mostly by official reports and other documents in Jack's file is far from auspicious.

It was 1976. A farmer was outside on his rural property not far from the Cranberry Wilderness when he saw a large animal. According to one newspaper account, the farmer immediately ran for his gun. He returned in time to see the animal attack one of his lambs. He claimed that he didn't realize the animal was a mountain lion until after he had shot it. He expressed concern that he might now be in trouble with the state.

If the article is accurate, the first verified West Virginia cougar sighting in decades sent a man running reflexively for his gun, and featured a cougar caught in the act of livestock predation.

Things went downhill from there.

Two days later another cougar was spotted near the same site. This second animal was resting under a stone ledge, apparently unconcerned with the crowd that began gathering. It appeared to be female and extremely pregnant.

The first official plan was to leave her alone. If she was an eastern cougar, the Endangered Species Act said she must not be harmed. Capture is particularly dangerous to a pregnant animal. As officials grappled with the problem, the cause of it all continued to rest quietly, now ringed by more than one hundred people, most local, some armed, and at least one with hunting dogs. Leaving her alone was clearly not going to fly.

For lack of a better plan, at about 1:00 A.M. she was darted. Now West Virginia DNR, which like Virginia, Missouri, and Arkansas lists the eastern cougar as extirpated, had both a dead and now a live cougar on its hands.

Another flurry of mail and phone calls ensued. Should she be released? If she was an Eastern cougar, she had to be. But where? In theory, near her capture site to maximize survival odds. But locals had promised they would kill her if given a second opportunity.

The argument was still going on three weeks later when, on May 7, a frustrated DNR official wrote to the U.S. Fish and Wildlife Service, the agency in charge of managing the federal Endangered Species Act: "We have no desire to keep this animal. Since this is the Service's cat, you should feel free to make whatever disposition of it you deem necessary. We would, however, like some indication as to when you will pick up the animal."

It's not clear from Jack's file what happened to the female, but the decision had been made that they were both probably FERCs, which released officials from the obligation of freeing her.

One factor in that decision was the female's apparent comfort near humans; another was the fact that both animals' front claws were more blunted than their hind claws, supposedly typical for an animal who has lived on a concrete pad. The animals' endoparasites were also found to be nonnative.

This all happened long before Jack's time. What would he do in that hot seat today?

"I'm not aware of any official plan. Right now if you were to call about a cougar, I hope I'd say leave it alone unless it's threatening you. Just because it's there doesn't mean we have to do anything about it."

He suspects this would not be popular. But if he's around long enough, he believes one day he'll get the chance to see if he actually says those words, and what happens after he does.

13

CINDY PAROLIN, 1996

Eleven-year-old Melissa Parolin loved riding horses. And she loved spending time with her mother, especially since time was something Cindy Parolin didn't usually have much of. Until recently Melissa's mother had juggled three jobs to pay off college loans, splitting her remaining energy among her husband and four children.

So on this August afternoon in 1996, Melissa didn't need the cool sun or high white clouds to make her smile. She sat straight-backed in the saddle, pretty Flicka's ears tipped in the direction of the base camp her father had picked out, from which the family would ride and explore for a glorious two weeks. And Mum led the way.

Melissa rode often at her grandparents' ranch near the tiny British Columbia town of Tulameen. In fact she couldn't even remember the first time she was lifted into a saddle. But the family had never gone on a horse camping trip before. Already they were miles from the ranch. Soon they would pass the last popular camping spots on Tulameen River Road. Then they'd have the woods to themselves.

Melissa was slim, brown-haired, and freckled, with gray eyes set wide in a round face. Nine-year-old Billy, blond and good-looking, rode ahead of her. Thirteen-year-old David rode beside her with the same wiry athleticism that made him a hotshot in the hockey rink. Cindy, in the lead, was dark-haired like her daughter. When she smiled, round cheeks crinkled her eyes nearly shut. Like everyone else, Melissa found it hard not to smile back. But the important thing about Mum was that her soft, round, five-feet-one-inch frame concealed a rock-solid will. There were no problems Mum couldn't solve.

All morning the family sauntered up the road, the cool air alive with jokes and laughter and bits of song. Before they had left the Parolin ranch, Grandma had said that Cindy should carry a gun on the day's ride. Melissa hadn't heard Mum's answer, but she wasn't troubled. Grandma was a worrier, always telling you to be careful about this or that. She probably thought she still lived in the wild and woolly frontier of her girlhood.

The plan had been for Melissa's dad, Les, to load a small mountain of camping supplies into the bed of his old Ford half-ton. With Les would ride Steven, six and too young for such a long horseback ride. A family friend would follow in Cindy's car. Cindy, juggling time as usual, needed the old Celica to drive into town for work several times during this adventure.

Meanwhile, Cindy and the three oldest children would ride more than twenty miles up seldom traveled Tulameen River Road. Les would meet them at midday with lunch, then drive ahead to set up camp at a cluster of run-down cabins he knew about, tucked back into the forest somewhere near road's end.

The day passed quickly, although the last few miles seemed much longer and dustier than the early ones. At 6:00 P.M. Melissa Parolin took a final sip of root beer and tossed away the can. She didn't usually litter and wondered absently why she had. Then she forgot about the candy that a can refund could buy. She was tired and still hungry: Dad hadn't brought lunch. Instead he'd arrived just a few minutes ago with nothing but candy bars and pop. One candy bar for a whole day's ride? She was going to eat lots of dinner, that was for sure.

Now Dad was pulling ahead in a haze of dust. Billy rode beside him, drafted to help set up camp. Steven, rescued from the truck and thrilled as only a six-year-old can be at such a magnificent turn of events, rode placid old Goomba in Billy's place. He chattered excitedly about nothing, which, since he was by far her favorite brother, was only a little irritating. Melissa noticed that his sneakers were untied. The laces dangled toward the stirrups, which his short legs couldn't reach.

The road lay in shadow. The early evening air shimmered with the delicate hum of mosquitoes. Melissa pulled her jean jacket from the saddle tiedowns and slipped it over her bare arms. Mum said camp was minutes away. This sounded good to Melissa.

Then movement caught her eye. Something was in the willows just off the trail. It was brown and hugged the ground. Coyote, maybe. That was neat. You didn't see coyotes every day. Mum and Steven, unaware, pulled abreast of it but the creature ignored them. It stared back down the road at Melissa. She stared back, puzzled. Coyotes were so shy. You mostly saw them running away. Then the ears and eyes flicked away from Melissa, lighting first on her mother, then Steven.

As though that stare prickled, the lead horses sidestepped nervously. Flicka stopped. Melissa could feel the big body tense between her legs. In the corner of her eye, she saw David's horse dance backward.

The creature had begun gliding onto the road. When its long tail emerged from the bush, Melissa understood that this was no coyote. She was looking at a creature she'd seen only in books and on TV: a mountain lion.

Flicka's growing tension told Melissa that in a few moments the horse would bolt. She had been thrown before. "This is going to hurt," she thought.

Then, almost absently, she realized she didn't have to be thrown. She dismounted, flipping the reins back over the animal's neck so the mare wouldn't trip when she bolted. Moments later Flicka was pounding away.

Meanwhile, the cougar had crossed the road toward where Cindy and Steven were struggling to calm their jittery horses. It padded straight to Goomba's side, then flew into the air. It seemed to float a moment before the little boy. Then it swiped a paw sideways. Melissa thought the motion looked like a person trying to clear a stack of books from a desk. The big paw missed the boy, however, and the cougar dropped lightly to the ground.

"Hold on, Steven. Mum's coming. Hold on," Mum chanted softly.

But terrified old Goomba shivered sideways, and Steven toppled toward the cat. He landed, rolled once, and regained his feet. They stood a moment facing one another, their heads almost on a level.

This time the boy was hard to miss. The cougar rose and stroked its front paws across his scalp. Instantly there was blood. A lot of blood.

Melissa doesn't remember what Steven would later describe, that the cougar knocked him facedown. And then, it seemed to Steven, it began clawing slits in his skin and inserting its teeth into the incisions, delicately lifting his scalp away.

Frozen, she stared at her mum, who had dismounted and was breaking a branch from a log. The decisive crack freed Melissa, allowing her to hurry forward. If Mum was doing something, maybe she could do something too.

Mum used the four-foot-long stick to jab the cougar's shoulder, trying to push it from Steven, or at least distract it. It ignored her. She jabbed more fiercely. The stick snapped in two.

Then Cindy Parolin did something nearly unimaginable: This soft city girl who had never physically attacked anything in her life threw herself full-length at the cat, rolled it off her son and, jamming her right forearm into its mouth, pinned it on its back beside the little boy. This made more sense to Melissa than anything that had happened so far.

The boy rose and stepped around his mother and the cat as though they weren't there. He walked to Melissa and sagged against her. She slipped her arms around him.

The boy's face was almost untouched. There was only one deep scratch across the nose. But his scalp was in tatters. Even Steven's mutilated head couldn't shake Melissa now. Everything was going to be all right. Mum was in control.

Her mother lay motionless, pressing the cat's head into the dirt. Melissa could see its slightly curved canines rest against the heavy fabric of Mum's oilskin riding jacket. The cat's front paws were planted against Cindy's chest. Its back legs were hidden beneath her body. Its tail lashed, but it lay otherwise still, staring up at its captor. It didn't look so big now.

David appeared, carrying a melon-sized rock. "Do you want me to drop this on his head?"

"No," said Cindy. "It'll make him mad."

David didn't drop the rock where he stood. He walked away to replace it exactly where he'd found it. Melissa wished he was smashing it onto the cougar instead, but like all the Parolin children, David had been raised to mind.

Watching their mother, perhaps both children ticked through their options. Les, a hunter and a cowboy, never went into the bush unarmed, but he and his gun were both in camp. There was no knife, either. And no club. There was only bloody little Steven, Mum with her arm jammed into a cougar's mouth, and a road that might remain empty for hours. The horses were gone, their hoof prints tattooed into the road's clay surface.

"Take Steven and go get your dad," said Cindy. She didn't look up.

Relieved to have a mission, Melissa lifted as much of Steven's weight as she could and began shuffling toward camp. Then it dawned on her: Every step toward Les left her mother more alone with that cougar. She glanced further up the road. David had already disappeared around the first bend. She turned to look back. Her mother still lay tensely atop the animal, which remained frozen except for the lashing tail. Everything was still under control. So why did her stomach feel like kneaded dough?

She turned and struggled up the road. Camp was minutes away, Mum had said just before the cougar appeared. Neither Melissa nor David knew exactly where, except that the cabins were down a steep hill and away from the road. But Mum's car wouldn't have been able to handle the sidetrack. It would be parked near the turnoff. When they found the car it would point to Dad, and he would save Mum.

That was when Melissa heard four or five long belly screams. It didn't sound like Mum it sounded like an animal in pain. Melissa's calm snapped. Suddenly she understood that things were far from under control.

She needed to go back, but she also needed to do what she was told—find her dad. She froze. It was too much. Then a small voice piped up from the circle of her arms.

"Can I have your hat?" it said.

"What? Why?"

"So you don't have to see my head," Steven answered earnestly. He had another reason, but he was too young to fit words to it. He could feel warmth slipping through the gashes in his head. He thought when all the warmth got out, he'd be dead. If he could trap that life-warmth in his big sister's hat, he might live.

Melissa's attention snapped dizzily from her mother's danger to her little brother's. All that blood. He was hurt bad.

She pulled her prized cowboy hat from her head and placed it in his hands. They shuffled on.

A few minutes later she heard a mumble, "I'm kind of tired. Can I sit down?" This sleepy voice sounded even less like excitable Steven. Melissa was getting tired, too. The boy's feet moved in front of her blunt-toed cowboy boots as though he were walking, but by now she supported nearly all his weight.

There were no sounds from behind. That was almost worse than the screaming. It made her wish she could pick up her brother and run, toward help but also away from whatever was back there.

"I feel tired. I have to sit down," the little voice came again. A new fear struck her: Could Steven be dying? It suddenly seemed clear to Melissa that a person missing so much scalp couldn't survive long. She guided him to a steep bank that might protect their backs.

"I have some raisins," said the small voice.

"Eat them," Melissa ordered. Food might lend him strength. Steven's wanting food might be his body telling him how to stay alive. "Eat them."

And one by one, the boy pinched the shriveled fruit into his mouth, his blood-streaked face impassive.

Melissa didn't think she could carry him anymore. But it wasn't safe to sit here, and Steven needed a doctor. She began to yell, "David? David, I need help."

A few minutes later, David jogged back around the bend. "I saw the car," he said. But he'd been unable to find the camp. He told his sister he'd yelled for Dad and then yelled repeatedly, "Les!" so Dad wouldn't think somebody else's kid was calling. He punched the car horn but it made no sound. He hunted for car keys, thinking he could drive back for Melissa and then Mum. There were none. Then he'd heard Melissa yell and returned.

There were two places left to try, he said. Beyond the car the right fork of the road led to an abandoned hard-rock mine. The left fork led to Myra Brewer's cabins. It was possible that the Parolin camp lay off one of those roads. It was also possible, though unlikely, that other people would be at the mine or at Myra's place.

David took his first good look at Steven then. The hat, he told his sister, should come off. It might get stuck to the wounds. Steven didn't resist as his big brother gently lifted it. Shocked by the flaps and folds of bloody scalp beneath, David found himself trying to push and pinch the mess back into place. The child did not object to this either.

They let Steven rest a bit more. When they could stand it no longer, each reached under an arm and lifted, letting Steven's feet shuffle on the road. Five minutes later they reached Cindy's car.

David pulled a cooler out of the passenger side and Steven crawled in, folding himself into a bundle on the seat. The older children told him he was safe. They told him not to lock the door so they could get in even if he fell asleep. They looked at each other, both knowing that it wasn't his falling asleep that they feared.

Between the front seats lay an open pack of chocolate-covered Wagon Wheels. David thought Steven shouldn't eat anything, but Melissa again hoped food would make him stronger. Besides, Steven loved food.

"You can have some," she blurted, gesturing at the cookies. Usually you couldn't shut Steven up, but he didn't say anything. He didn't reach for the cookies either. Melissa closed the door.

The children began yelling for their father. He had to be close. Maybe he'd hear two voices where he hadn't heard one.

But their only answer was a shushing sound as wind tangled in the upper branches of the pines. The slanted evening light pooled cool shadows on the road. It would be dark soon, and Mum was still alone with that cougar. Or worse, it had escaped her and watched them now from the leafy darkness that walled the road.

Someone needed to run up to the mine, David said. One of them should stay with Steven, but neither could stand to go alone. As they jogged uphill together, neither noticed the twin tire ruts, faint and screened by brush, that veered left and sharply downhill a hundred feet from the car. Nor did they notice them as they panted back down minutes later. Their mother needed them to return with help, but Melissa and David had so far failed to find any.

Fifty-one-year-old Jim Manion and his wife, Karen, had arrived at their cabin Sunday night to begin a quiet vacation. Jim was tall. His angular features, stained-wood skin, and dark eyes bespoke his native Salish ancestry. His leg braces told of determination: After a tree fell on a much younger Jim, he had been told he'd never walk again. Now he wore shoes with heavy, stiff soles. Weighty braces ran up his calves to stabilize numb and mostly paralyzed feet. But, by God, he walked.

At forty-eight, Karen was short and blonde. Children liked her, perhaps because she liked them. In fact, she liked to think she had preserved in herself the best qualities of a kid. She hated shoes so she seldom wore any. Barefoot now, she sat on the porch of the tiny, rough-cut lumber cabin Jim and two brothers-in-law had built.

Then they both heard something. Karen lowered her book to stare at the wall of forest. Jim tried to concentrate on the distant sounds. Children shouting, he thought. But you couldn't make out the words. What were kids doing out here on a Monday evening? It would soon be dark. He should probably go check it out, make sure nothing was wrong.

A few minutes later, as Jim returned from the outhouse, he saw a figure jogging into camp. He recognized the oldest Parolin boy. He didn't know the family except to nod at, but his grandparents and Les's had both moved to the area over a century ago. Jim's aunt, Myra Brewer, and Les's mother were friends.

The panting boy's story would have been hard to believe except for its matter-of-fact delivery. David sounded like he'd spent the last ten minutes arranging words into the most efficient order. Their mother needed help fighting off a cougar. Little Steven was safe with Melissa in a car but he'd been hurt by the cat. And David couldn't find his father, who was supposed to be nearby.

The boy's unflinching eyes pulled at Jim's heart more than tears could have.

The tall man clumped into the cabin and began throwing things onto the bed: towels for bandages, flour to slow bleeding, a jug of water to clean wounds, shells, and his old 12-gauge shotgun.

The shotgun always leaned against the cabin wall. No longer used for hunting, it was simply a noisemaker to frighten off the occasional curious bear. This mountain lion was probably long gone, but, just in case, Jim pulled the plug so the old shotgun would hold five shells instead of three.

Jim also threaded his bayonet-style hunting knife onto his belt. Then he scooped up the supplies and ran to the truck. Into the Chevy's back seat went his cow dog Kala and his brother-in-law's expensive young bird dog, a golden retriever named Trem which the couple was babysitting. Jim's mind, ticking in high gear, could think of ways dogs might be useful. He could hear Karen doing her kid magic by the truck. Hugging the boy with one arm, she asked questions and listened gravely to the answers.

———

Melissa heard an engine. She had been coaxing Steven with boxed juice and cookies. She had read somewhere that badly injured people shouldn't be allowed to sleep, so she talked. She told him everything would be fine even though she was now certain he was dying. The little boy seemed barely able to speak. All he would say was his refrain from their scary walk to the car, "I'm so tired."

After they had returned from the old mine, David had asked her to run up the remaining fork toward old Myra Brewer's place. He was tired. He'd already run a lot farther than she had.

"I can't go, David. I just can't," Melissa had begged. She was sick of being scared. All she could think about was climbing into Mum's car, slamming the door, being safe. So they'd agreed that David would run one more time, as far as Myra's, then come back if he found no help. Nothing was said about what they'd do after that. What was there to say?

Melissa had climbed into the driver's seat beside Steven. A few minutes after David left, the urge to pee got so strong that she reluctantly got out. But once she was standing, the feeling faded and she realized it was just fear pooling in her gut. She dove gratefully back into the car.

The white Chevy roaring up the road toward her was a beautiful sight. Melissa jumped out and waved her arms. Two adults emerged with David. They were vaguely familiar.

The woman headed straight for Steven. She looked at the gelled red mess of his head, then began checking the boy for less obvious wounds. Melissa couldn't hear her questions, but Steven's answers were tiny yeses and nos. When the woman backed out of the car, she seemed relieved. She said the bleeding had mostly stopped, the wounds looked worse than they were, and Steven would be all right. Then, before Melissa could relax into the reassuring authority of adults, the woman told her she would have to stay with Steven again, alone.

Karen Manion and her tall, stern-faced husband, Jim, needed David to find Cindy for them. But someone had to keep Steven from moving around. Melissa didn't want to be left alone again. She bit back the words she wanted to yell, "No. Don't go. Don't leave me alone. You just got here."

She knew her disappointment showed because the woman hugged her. "We'll be back. We'll be back as soon as we can," she said.

Melissa climbed into the still-warm seat and shut the door. The truck bounced away and responsibility settled on her again. Beyond the window, she watched light slowly fade until the sky was dusky and deep. Time passed.

Then the roar of the truck again. Melissa jumped out and anxiously scanned the cab, but only Jim, Karen, and David got out. Her question stuck in her throat a moment, then came out fast. "Where's Mum?"

They told her a man with a blue van was taking Cindy to the hospital. Melissa relaxed a little. Mum was hurt—she had been braced for that ever since the screams—but hospitals fixed people who were hurt.

Karen explained that she and Jim would take the Parolin children to the hospital, too. Jim wrote on a piece of paper, "Your wife has been injured. She was attacked by a cougar. Steven is seriously injured. They're being taken to the hospital."

He propped the note on the Celica's steering wheel and closed the door. Melissa had another question, but they were loaded up and headed toward Princeton before she could make herself ask. "How bad is she?"

Nobody answered although Melissa gave them lots of time.

"How bad is she?" she asked again, louder and shriller.

David sounded reluctant, "It's fifty-fifty, Melissa. She's hurt pretty bad. Isn't that right, Jim?"

Fifty-fifty? What was that supposed to mean?

The ninety-minute drive to town was dreamlike. Steven rode in the woman's lap, his head wrapped in towels. Melissa was squeezed in back with David and the two dogs. Somehow the woman had gotten David talking about the movie *Star Wars*.

"Maybe we all know a song," she said, and the next thing Melissa knew they were actually singing. At one point David stopped in the middle of a verse he couldn't recall. A small voice piped up from beneath the turban, finishing the line. Everyone laughed. For a grateful moment, Melissa forgot about fifty-fifty.

As Melissa stared beyond the adults' heads, she caught a glitter of silver and brown—her soda pop can from that afternoon. She even thought she saw a tiny tongue of dampness where the last drops of root beer had seeped out. She remembered how it had felt to toss the can aside, as though nothing she might do this day mattered all that much. She thought, then and years later, how odd it was that such a little thing, an empty pop can beside a dirt road, would stick so jarringly in her memory. If the day had ended as it was supposed to, she suspected she would have ridden by that pop can two weeks later, heading home with her entire, uninjured family, and never noticed it.

And how had the day really ended? What had David and these two adults found when they returned for Mum? Melissa, caught up in fifty-fifty and the memory of screams, didn't ask. Not that night, and not for a long time. And the stern-faced man who knew the whole, incredible story thought it kinder not to offer.

14
ANSWERS

Jim Manion waited years to tell the Parolin kids what happened to their mom on the Tulameen River Road that night in 1996. They had a right. But he needed them to ask and they didn't. The newspapers did, but he found he didn't want to talk to them. By his code, a man didn't help his neighbor in order to draw attention to himself.

This was not a story about a big, bad cougar, either. It was about heroes, and the heroes were those brave kids and their braver mom. They were the ones who had paid. The newspaper stories should celebrate them.

But the events of that Monday evening did not grow indistinct. Three years later he spent one long summer day reliving them for this book, in hopes that the Parolin kids would, when they were ready, decide to read it.

Jim, Karen, and the boy roared away from the Manion cabin to find the dusty Celica right where David had said it would be, more proof the boy was steady. While Karen tended the injured child, Jim examined the Parolin kids' faces. No tears. No panic. Even Steven, who looked like he'd been scalped, was dry-eyed.

The child shouldn't be moved. The bleeding might start again. Besides, Jim couldn't shake a vision of Cindy Parolin ripped to pieces in the road. If he could, he'd protect the kids from that sight.

But he needed a guide. Minutes later, Jim and Karen scanned the road from the cab of the white Chevy. Beside them sat David.

Pine- and willow-lined, rutted and rock-strewn, each turn in the road looked the same to Jim. He drove slowly. Soon they would lose daylight, but how would the boy recognize the spot if Jim rushed? A mile from Cindy's car, Jim noticed disturbed gravel in the road. He knew cougars dragged their kills into cover. Could the disturbances be drag marks? But he counseled himself not to jump to conclusions and said nothing. Let the boy concentrate, he told himself. Moments later, David pointed through the windshield.

"Right up here," he said.

David jumped out before the truck came to a full stop. Karen and both dogs followed. They ran up the road, yelling, "Mum!" and "Cindy!" Jim stood by the truck, studying the road and ditch bank. He saw horses' tracks in the clay, spaced close as though made by slow-moving animals. Then milling confusion. Then the hoofprints headed the opposite way, wide-spaced, at full gallop. The boy had found the spot, all right.

Jim was still staring at those prints when he heard a woman's voice. It said clearly, calmly, "Over here."

Cindy Parolin was alive. Jim realized he hadn't believed she would be.

The voice came from somewhere behind him. He stared intently, but the road was empty and off both sides he saw only willow thicket and shadow.

Deeply uneasy, Jim called David and Karen back to the truck. Cindy was alive, but she wasn't strolling out onto the road. He asked Karen to turn the truck around and drive toward the voice. Armed with the old shotgun, he would walk.

Jim moved forward cautiously. Cindy must be injured and hurrying might save her life. But if the cat was still around, it could end his. He watched the bank below the road. A cougar wouldn't pull a heavy meal uphill.

"Cindy, is the cat in the area?" he called.

Her answer came immediately, small but almost conversational: "Yes."

The voice had originated near the road, some twenty paces ahead. He moved forward again, even more slowly.

There was no blood on the road, no sign of struggle in the brush or down the four-foot ditch bank, only those scuffed bits of gravel he had noticed from the truck.

"Is the cat with you?"

"Yes."

Yes? It seemed unbelievable, but he couldn't doubt that calm voice. He was close enough to pinpoint it this time, a thick tangle of willow twenty feet in diameter just below the ditch bank in a grassy meadow. Jim tried to make his eyes push leaves and twigs aside, but all he saw was green and gray shadow. He stepped forward.

Then an electric tingle ran up his neck to his hairline: A new-looking riding jacket lay on the road bank, collar pointed toward him. It seemed as though it had been carefully placed there.

This fit none of the scenarios Jim had been constructing. The kids had told him she was wearing her jacket when the cat attacked. He'd been glad to hear it, thinking the oilskin would protect her. The marks in the road seemed to say that Cindy had been dragged here from the original attack site a hundred yards away. So how did the jacket end up before him, clean and neatly folded in half? For some reason, this unwieldy detail bothered him almost as much as the thought that a cougar might be—no, *was*—crouched paces away.

Jim heard the truck pull up.

"Cindy, is it right next to you?"

"Yes."

Jim drew back. He needed to think. He heard Karen, the boy, and the golden retriever on the road above him. His cow dog, Kala, had almost certainly dived back into the truck at the sight of the shotgun in his hand. That was good: She'd be safe.

"Karen, put Trem in the truck," he yelled. The golden was young and not completely trained. It also wasn't his. When he heard the truck door slam, he turned his attention back to Cindy. What kind of reassurance would he want if he was her?

"Cindy, we have your kids," he said. "They're all OK."

Silence. He wished he could see her. He wished he could see the cat. When the voice came again, it was smaller still but just as calm: "I'm dying."

Jim eased forward. He leaned for a different angle, peering deep into the thicket. This time he saw her. Her legs pointed toward him from ten feet away. They looked OK. He scanned up her body. Her clothing wasn't ripped. Jim felt hope rising, despite Cindy's words and his own growing awareness that the air was saturated with the iron tang of blood.

He leaned in from a slightly different angle and saw her head. The heavy shadows made it hard to tell for sure, but there seemed to be something badly wrong with her face.

And then he saw the cat. It was a shock, even though he had thought he'd believed Cindy. Its chest was pressed against her right shoulder, its dark face immediately above hers. It stared at Jim. How had he not seen those eyes?

The sight of the cat was almost a relief. Now Jim could forget the weird vision of that neatly arranged jacket, the woman's damaged face, and her gentle admonition that she was out of time. He had a mission: He had to get that cat away from Cindy Parolin. And he had to do it before daylight faded completely.

Jim knew cougars were strong and fast, and this one had overpowered two people already, but he didn't think his mission was a difficult one. Unlike Cindy, he was armed.

He raised the shotgun. Then he realized he couldn't fire: Brush obscured most of the cat's body. The old Remington 12-gauge was loaded with light shot which even at close range might be deflected by twigs into Cindy's arm, shoulder, and face. Some rescuer he'd be if he killed the woman he came to save.

He needed the cat to move, to present a better target. He reached back, grabbed two fist-sized rocks, and threw one into the brush above the cat. It didn't twitch, just beamed those huge eyes at him.

The next rock hit the cougar in the neck hard enough that Jim heard the meaty thud. Still it didn't move.

He took another step forward and aimed the shotgun above the cat's head. The weapon crashed. Leaves and twigs rained onto the animal. Unbelievably, it remained a statue. Jim was beginning to get angry, but he was also fascinated. What kind of animal didn't flinch at the discharge of a firearm four feet away?

And more important, what now? Cindy hadn't spoken again. He could feel David's eyes on his back. He was pretty sure the cat's eyes were still glued to him as well. But if he had to choose, he'd face the cat before he'd say to a thirteen-year-old boy, "I give up. I don't know what to do. Your mother will just have to die."

His last options, neither very attractive, were to use his brother-in-law's expensive young bird dog as bait, or throw himself at the cat. He'd start with the dog.

"Karen, let Trem out," he called.

"What do you mean, let him out? You told me to put him in."

"Just let him out."

Jim wasn't sure what to ask the approaching dog for. But it occurred to him that if Trem circled the thicket, the cat might rise for a better look or even give chase. Either way, Jim would get his shot.

"Circle, Trem," he said, for lack of a better command, and waved his arm vaguely as if the gesture should mean something to the young dog.

The golden stared at him a moment. Then, amazingly, he wheeled to trot a big circle around the willows, leaving Jim's right hand and returning to his left, exactly as Jim had envisioned. But the cougar didn't move, didn't even glance away from the man.

Now Jim noticed what looked like a rabbit run entering the willows from behind. It led straight to the cat. Jim hated to sacrifice this obedient dog.

"Circle, Trem," he said reluctantly, waving his arm as before. And the dog began again to trot around the willow thicket. When the flashes of yellow that were Trem reached the rabbit run, Jim tightened his grip on the shotgun, silently apologized to the dog, and yelled, "Get 'em!"

The dog wheeled into the tunnel and charged the cougar's back, but Jim never got a shot. The cougar spun so fast Jim registered only blurred motion. Then it was flying at Trem, screened by the tangled willows.

Trem was barely smaller than the cougar. He was the color of chamois; the cat was brown with a darker stripe down its back. The force of the cat's attack somersaulted them up the rabbit tunnel and five or six times across the clearing, a silent gold and brown knot. When the tumbling stopped, Trem seemed surprised to find himself on top. The dog hesitated an instant, then leaped free and bolted for the road.

Jim heard Karen yell, "He's in the truck," but he didn't have time to be relieved for his brother-in-law's good dog. He was going to get his shot now, and he'd better not miss: With a boneless lope, the cat was out in the open and coming for him.

Jim envisioned what would happen. As it approached, the cougar would leap a log that lay crosswise in the clearing forty feet away. This would expose its chest and neck. At forty feet, as Jim well knew, the old shotgun's pattern was fifteen inches across. Jim stood in a slight depression, just right of the thicket where Cindy lay. With his shotgun at his hip, the barrel would line up perfectly with the cat's exposed chest.

"I really can't miss," he told himself and knew it to be true.

When it reached the log, Jim reminded himself, "Squeeze, don't pull," and contracted his forefinger. Nothing.

"The gun's jammed," he yelled at Karen. Previous experience with the old weapon told him what had happened. The pump had slipped back a couple inches, preventing the firing mechanism from engaging. It would take a bare second to jack the pump, but in that second, his attention would be diverted from the approaching cat. Now that he'd seen how far a cougar could move in the blink of an eye, that instant of inattention seemed foolish. He had always heard cougars were quick, but Jim Manion hadn't known anything could move fast enough to literally blur.

Jim kept the useless gun aimed at the cat, mostly from habit, but he funneled all his energy into making his gaze a physical force. That cat had been staring at him nonstop. Fine. Two could play that game. Jim's grandfather had been a guide and trapper: Maybe the old man had told him this would work. But whether from distant memory or gut instinct, he knew that if he stared hard enough the cougar would stop before reaching him.

Ten feet away, it did. Eyes locked, man and cat stood motionless. A second stretched to ten, thirty, sixty.

Jim again considered snapping the gun up, jacking the pump, and hoping the firing mechanism would engage. The trouble was, if it didn't the cat would be on him. He was certain of it.

He decided to back away. He'd do it smoothly, slowly. First he reached to his hip to unsnap his knife. The cat didn't seem to care what

Jim did with his hands, only with his eyes.

Jim's braces and thick-soled boots prevent his ankles from flexing. Nerve damage from the long-ago logging accident means he can't tell whether he's on stable ground or loose rock. Practice has taught him to maintain balance by sensations in his knees, where he still has feeling. But that more distant checkpoint means Jim often can't know he's on unstable ground until he begins to stumble.

Jim was pretty sure a momentary loss of balance would bring the cat. As he backed into the four-foot-high bank below the road, he remembered what it had looked like coming down: loose gravel, big rocks, and a little weedy vegetation.

He placed each foot carefully, digging with his heel, listening for rock sounds, then committing his weight, grateful each time it held. The cat stepped forward a little more slowly than Jim retreated, as though their stares made an elastic but unbreakable band.

One last step and Jim's knees told him he was on level ground. He'd made it to the road. Now he was able to move more quickly, gliding backward twenty feet or so to the truck and sidling behind the open driver's door, all before the cat appeared on the road.

Jim didn't realize until then that they had company. The cougar faced Jim, Karen, David, two dogs, a pickup truck—and now a blue van, from which a young man hopped, calling "What's going on?" When he saw the approaching cougar, he jumped back into his vehicle and slammed the door.

Jim wasn't a cougar hunter, but he had been born and raised in these parts and he knew what everyone knew: Cougars were shy, despite their formidable strength and speed. That this one, now so outnumbered, merely stopped and stood in the road amazed him. It should have evaporated like a water droplet on a sun-struck rock.

After a few moments, though, the animal finally seemed ready to back down. It turned and began to walk away down the middle of the road, its stride slow and deliberate. Jim flashed suddenly angry. He jacked the pump of his shotgun, muttering under his breath, "You're not getting away with this. I'm going to fill your butt with buckshot and you're going to know about hurt."

Aware he was not behaving rationally, he stepped from behind the door and strode after the cat. The cougar wheeled around. Almost gleeful now, Jim aimed as he walked. At twenty feet, he told himself, the cat would drop into its crouch and prepare to leap. When its chest touched the road, Jim would fire.

Once again it happened as Jim had foreseen. As Jim approached, the cat sank to the road, tensing. Jim squeezed the trigger. This time the old shotgun roared.

What happened next still awes him: At such close range, Jim knew, his shotgun would blow a hole through plywood. He had expected the cat to be slung backward by the impact. But for one frozen instant, it didn't even flinch. Then, as if the dirt road had become unbearably hot, the cougar uncoiled and shot straight into the air. For a moment it seemed to hang, paws dangling three feet off the road. Then it dropped back, only to uncoil again in a sailing arc that took it perhaps twenty feet to the road's edge. Three more weightless leaps and it was gone.

Jim couldn't help thinking this was no normal cougar. Could it be normal for a cougar to crouch unflinching when a shotgun discharged right over its head? To face four humans, two dogs, and two vehicles? To execute such amazing leaps when Jim knew it must be badly wounded? To attack a grown woman in the first place and then crouch over her even when faced with an armed man and a dog?

Karen had already crawled into the thicket. She was crouched beside Cindy, yelling, "We're here, Cindy. We're people."

Jim thought fast about that barely glimpsed face, and called David. He was relieved when the boy came running toward the front of the truck instead of toward his mother. Good, obedient boy.

"Listen, do you know how to operate this?" he said, holding out his shotgun.

"Yes."

"Show me."

The boy did. Jim glanced at the willow thicket and positioned David so he couldn't easily see down there.

"Stay here. And if the lion comes back, shoot it," ordered Jim.

"OK."

"You know your mother's been hurt very badly?"

"Yes."

"We're talking fifty-fifty here, David. Do you understand?"

The boy nodded. Jim hoped it wasn't a lie.

Karen was still shouting into Cindy's face as Jim threaded into the thicket. The van driver was there, too. He seemed upset.

"Why are you doing that to her?" he said.

"I sure as hell don't want her to think I'm that cougar," she snapped. "I want her to know she won't be hurt anymore."

Jim smelled something faint and unpleasant. It tugged at an old memory he couldn't quite grab hold of.

Then he saw Cindy's face. He took in a staring eye and the bloody socket where the other had been. A mouth so badly ripped it was hard to imagine it had spoken those clear words to him. Like her son, the woman had been partially scalped. Had the cougar done this while Jim stood up on the road, while Cindy spoke to him? The thought made him nearly sick with sympathy. Karen had stopped yelling. Her look and a tiny shake of her head told him the rest.

Then the memory came: a bad car wreck when Jim was nineteen, a friend suddenly dead beside him and a vague, putrid smell that Jim would later decide was the stinking signature of death itself. Karen had left the cabin barefoot, as usual. Jim would notice late that night that she was coated to the ankles in bloody mud, but the remembered smell wasn't the smell of blood. It lay beneath that metallic sharpness like a shadow.

They decided quickly that the boy didn't need to know yet. They'd act as though Cindy was alive and send her body ahead in the van. Jim, Karen, and the children would follow in Jim's truck. Those children had the rest of their lives to be motherless. Let them have her for a few more hours.

As the three adults carried their load onto the road, Jim blocked David's view with his body, but the effort was unnecessary: The boy was doing as he'd been told. He was intently watching the forest edge. Maybe he saw through the charade, because he didn't ask if he could ride with his mother. Or maybe he was just too tired to do anything other than follow directions.

It was nearly dark by the time the van drove off, headed toward

Princeton with Cindy's body. At 10:00 P.M. at Princeton General Hospital where Cindy Parolin had worked, she was officially pronounced dead.

Meanwhile Jim turned his truck back toward the Celica. They rounded up the two younger children and left a note for their father. As he slid behind the wheel, Jim glanced at Karen. She held the little boy, Steven, in her lap, cradling his head in her right arm. Jim could see blood beginning to soak through the towels. Steven, David, and Melissa had been through so much. Jim felt as proud and protective of them as if they had been his own.

A few moments later, Melissa asked the question he'd been dreading. "How bad is she?"

Jim silently begged David to answer.

"How bad is she?" Melissa repeated. Jim could hear the tension in her voice. Silence stretched. They don't have to know this yet, Jim thought. We shouldn't have to tell them.

Finally, David spoke. "It's fifty-fifty, Melissa. She's hurt pretty bad. Right, Jim?"

Jim silently thanked the boy.

Late that night with Steven safely in a hospital bed, Melissa and David were told Cindy Parolin had died on the way to the hospital.

For a moment, standing in the waiting room, Melissa felt hot anger. Why did Mum have to save Steven? Why had she let the cat kill her?

In the next moment, she remembered her mother telling an angry, crying brother a few months before, "I don't ever want to lose any of you."

And she ached with sudden pride. Her mother had meant it: She had died rather than lose a child.

That same night, officials followed a set of tracks to a dead cougar. Jim's old shotgun had done fatal damage after all. At sixty-three pounds, the young mountain lion was half the weight of its victim. Adults attacked by full-sized cougars have fought them off barehanded. Those who, like Cindy Parolin, attack cougars to rescue another nearly always walk away unscathed. Why was this woman dead?

Stop a moment and think. Cindy was wearing her riding jacket when Melissa last saw her. How did it end up laid neatly on the ground? If she was overpowered when Melissa heard screams, how is it she was still alive an hour later when the Manions and David arrived?

The answer that makes the most sense is that Cindy did walk away. If Jim really saw drag marks on the road, they were laid after she placed that jacket on the ground.

When two cougars fight, the smaller one nearly always loses. Often it dies. When Cindy charged the young cougar, it was intimidated by Cindy's attack and superior size. Once in a vulnerable position the animal was also almost certainly restrained by the fact that it was outnumbered four to one. Though it was powerful enough to escape at any time, it lay passive beneath Cindy with her arm in its jaws, sharp teeth resting against her coat.

At some point after the children left, the cat simply closed those jaws.

And when Cindy screamed and reacted, it escaped.

What then?

Perhaps believing it had fled, she removed the jacket to examine her injured arm, then forgot it as she hurried down the road after her children. The rest of the story we can never know, except that something finished her transformation in the cat's eyes from competitor to prey—because it had not left. It was watching. Perhaps she sat for a moment to tend her wounds. Sitting, she appeared vulnerable. Perhaps she went back for something lost in the struggle and bent to pick it up. Perhaps she saw the cat and ran, no longer brave without a child to save.

However it happened, when Cindy Parolin became prey, she lost. But that came after she had already won.

15

HOW SAFE IS YOUR CHILD?

When I spoke with Melissa Parolin, she was fourteen. She had clear gray eyes and an unflinching gaze. She described the events that stole her mother simply but vividly, as if they were still before her. At fourteen she still loved horses. She still cried for her mum.

Imagine looking into those sad eyes, knowing you believe cougars have a right to exist, knowing that belief has a blood price, and knowing you didn't pay it and this child, who isn't old enough yet to know what she believes, did.

What do you say to her?

The moment crystallized what is irresolvable for me about the calculus of cougar attack.

Every parent that recreates with his children in cougar country accepts a tiny risk. But, despite what happened to Cindy Panolin, the risk is almost never to the parent. Less than half of recent attack victims are children, but that statistic masks this one: When a cougar singles somebody out of a mixed-age group, it chooses a child.

The cougar that walked into a campground in British Columbia's Okanagan Valley in 1993 encountered a boy and his father panning gold. It leapt on the boy. So did the cougar who, in May 2006, crossed paths with a boy walking hand-in-hand with his father on a hiking trail near Boulder, Colorado. And so did the cougar who, on the bank of

Washington's Dungeness River in 1994, found a five-year-old and his dad throwing rocks in the water.

And, of course, the cougar that killed Cindy Parolin initially overlooked her, as well as her two older children. It attacked her youngest son, even though he was on horseback.

Statistically, the likeliest victim of a cougar attack is a boy. He's older than four, but younger than twelve. He's rarely alone when attacked, a fact that saves his life. Most of his wounds, concentrated around the head and neck, occur as the cougar tries to drag him away, just as it would a deer. No matter how fast rescuers move, the cougar has moved much faster. The child's injuries are serious.

When Robert Anderson climbed down a sandbar to the edge of Idaho's Salmon river, briefly leaving his eleven-year-old son Joel playing with a friend above him, he almost immediately heard his boy scream. He scrambled back up the bank to see a cougar biting Joel on the head and arm. Robert charged, letting his momentum power a punch to the cougar's nose that rolled it off the boy. It righted itself and faced him, snarling. He kicked sand into its eyes until it ran away. Robert had responded quickly, but Joel still needed eighty stitches.

Cougars seem to find children utterly compelling. Sheba, the captive-born cougar at the Fund for Animals shelter east of San Diego tends to ignore adults but likes to stalk children who walk the path around her grassy pen. She is never hungry, has never hunted, has never killed anything in her life.

Judy Underdahl learned just how powerful that attraction can be the day she cajoled her family into detouring through a Rapid City, South Dakota, animal park called Bear Country.

Judy had stopped the motor home to photograph several cougars lying under a tree. They seemed as bored and sleepy as her father Pete dozing in the back seat.

"They look like they're dead," she said to her mother Hazel. She handed Hazel the camera. "Will you clean your lens?"

"I wanna see the cougars," shouted Judy's two-year-old son Jason as he jumped onto the upholstered engine cover beside her.

At the toddler's shout, one of the cougars pricked its ears, eyed the boy, and then came electrically alive, sprinting to Judy's window. Its front paws thumped against the side of the motor home.

"It's coming in," Judy whispered, but no one heard her. Often unnerved by cows and even cats and dogs, Judy was terrified by the cougar's huge unblinking eyes and its loud purring. "It's coming in," she said again.

She tried to shake it off by goosing the motor home forward, which jarred open the sliding window beside her. In an instant the cat had vaulted in, scrambled over Judy, knocked Jason on his back, and pinned him to the engine cover.

When Judy grabbed for her son, the cougar bit her hand and flung it aside. The motor home crashed to a stop against a fence. Hazel cowered back against the passenger door, shouting, "Get a knife, get a knife."

Instead, Grandpa Pete tried to choke the cougar. It bit him, too, then went back to Jason.

Pete jerked open a drawer and rushed forward, thrusting the kitchen knife at Hazel.

She hesitated, took it, then plunged the blade into the cougar's chest just behind its left leg. She kept stabbing until the cougar dropped the wounded boy and crawled onto the driver's seat to die.

We tend to think children are protected by the presence of adults, but statistics do not support this. Few child victims of cougars have been alone when attacked. On July 31, 1998, at a day camp near Missoula, Montana, six-year-old Dante Swallow, the smallest kid in camp, was shuffling up a hill at the end of a long line of hikers. He had fallen a few steps behind sixteen-year-old Aaron, the youngest counselor.

"There's a mountain lion," said the six-year-old matter-of-factly.

When Aaron turned to look, he first saw what appeared to be dog paws reaching up from behind the boy. Then something slammed Dante down, face first. When the animal locked its jaws on the boy's head, Aaron saw the eyes of a cat. He flashed on an old story: a boy snatched from his tricycle and killed by a cougar on the nearby Flathead Indian reservation.

Galvanized, Aaron rushed toward the cougar, kicking dirt in its face. It hooked its claws into Dante and began to drag him away.

Aaron followed, booting the cat in the ribs until it shifted off the boy. Then Aaron stepped forward, straddling Dante just as the cougar had, glaring just as the cougar had. The cougar feinted, then reached between Aaron's legs to grab at the boy. Aaron kicked hard again, this time driving the instep of his worn-out running shoe into the cat's snout. It jumped up the road bank, then stopped ten feet away to stare intently at Aaron. Aaron charged. A flick of the tail and the cougar was gone.

Dante is fine. The hero of the story, however, slept in his parents' room for three weeks. In his dreams, the boy was so little, the cougar so large.

Lila Lifely, another camp counselor, saved her young charge, too. But then she had to save her again—and again, as in a bad horror movie.

After hiking from YWCA Camp Thunderbird on the south end of Vancouver Island to a peak known as Crow's Nest, Lila and her handful of girls dropped their packs to celebrate the summit. The girls were playing in a nearby clearing when Lila heard the first screams.

"Wild cat!" shrieked one girl as she fled past Lila. "It's mauling Alyson!"

Lila raced to the little clearing. A cougar was dragging ten-year-old Alyson Parker away by the head. Lila hit the cat on the forehead with a three-foot branch. It faded into the bushes.

She dropped to her knees beside Alyson. The girl was conscious and surprisingly calm. Her head wounds didn't look too bad, all things considered. Relieved, Lila started for her pack to get first aid gear. Alyson moaned and Lila looked back. The cougar had returned. It crouched over Alyson's head. Lila broke a four-foot-long segment from a hollow log and clobbered the cat again. It shot away.

Lila whipped off her T-shirt and bandaged Alyson's head with it. She had to have help, but didn't dare leave. In desperation, she covered the child with a sleeping bag and heaped brush over that. Then she climbed a tree to holler for help. There she could keep an eye on Alyson and stay out of the cat's reach. The rest of the girls cowered in a group on the mountain's summit.

When the camp director arrived with help more than an hour later, the cat had not returned. But as she knelt beside Alyson, the girls screamed again. The cougar was crawling through the brush toward the injured child. This time, shouting was sufficient to scare the cougar away long enough to get Alyson evacuated.

Millions of families go hiking every year without mishap. Rambunctious kids stray from the group and return, energized and confident to explore again. Statistics say the drive to the trailhead is by several orders of magnitude the riskiest part of the trip. But as one parent explained to me after reading cougar warnings during a 2006 visit to Yosemite National Park, it's not the level of the risk that is disturbing. It's the nature of the risk.

On July 17, 1997, Dave and Kathy Miedema brought their two children, ten-year-old Mark and his younger sister Rachel, to Colorado's Rocky Mountain National Park for a hike up the popular seven-mile trail to Cascade Falls.

The Miedemas and another family hit the trail a little after noon. They hiked past a paper sign posted at the trailhead:

WARNING!
MOUNTAIN LIONS
FREQUENTING THIS AREA
-BE ALERT-
SOLO HIKING AND JOGGING
NOT RECOMMENDED,
SUPERVISE CHILDREN CLOSELY!
THIS IS MOUNTAIN LION HABITAT
MOUNTAIN LIONS ARE BEAUTIFUL AND POTENTIALLY
DANGEROUS LARGE CATS THAT OCCUR IN THE PARK. ALTHOUGH
RARELY OBSERVED AND NOT USUALLY A THREAT TO PEOPLE,
HAZARDOUS ENCOUNTERS HAVE OCCURRED. UNSUPERVISED CHILDREN
AND LONE ADULTS ARE ESPECIALLY AT RISK. INQUIRE AT VISITOR
CENTERS FOR SAFE PRACTICES WHEN TRAVELING IN THE PARK.

Mark and Rachel were learning their parents' love of the high country. The family hiked and camped so often their neighbors referred to them as "nature people." On hikes, Mark played in every stream. Something would catch his eye as he walked and he would jump off the trail to take a closer look. Other times he would run ahead to hide, then pop out from behind trees at his family, a broad smile cracking his freckled face.

At Cascade Falls, the family snacked on trail mix and granola bars. Their friends had turned back earlier. After a while the Miedemas began the hike back as well. It was about 3:30 P.M. Mark was up to his usual explorations and nowhere to be seen. At one point Kathy and Dave met a backpacker who said the boy was three to four minutes ahead of them.

While Mark was doing his thing on that warm afternoon, an eighty-eight pound pregnant cougar was doing hers. Moving along a ridge through thick aspens, she was in the right kind of terrain to find deer. What she found instead was Mark.

The first thing Mark's father saw a few minutes later were the boy's skinny legs lying across the trail, his black socks and sneakers unusually still. It could have been another of Mark's pranks, but for some reason there was a deer standing close to his son. Or what he thought was a deer. And then it picked Mark up by the head and began dragging him down the trail.

Kathy saw it too. Both charged, screaming. The cougar dropped Mark and fled uphill into the trees. They ran to the motionless boy. He had no pulse. They performed CPR, soon helped by a nurse who happened along. Mark's heart fluttered once and quit again. They breathed for him and made his silent heart pump blood for nearly an hour. Then EMTs arrived to take over. Dave and Kathy gave their boy up to the coroner a little after 5:30. The cougar returned to the scene later that evening, coming within fifteen yards of a park ranger. The cat was treed and killed a mile from the site.

The coarse hairs found on his hands made the coroner think Mark had tried to fight back. But Mark was a fifty-pound boy facing an animal that killed two-hundred-pound deer for a living.

Two years later, Kathy's brother says that Kathy was still doubting her decision to let Mark run ahead, as he loved to do, and encounter the world at his own speed. She wrestled with her faith in God.

"We are slowly healing, although sometimes we take one step forward and two backwards," Dave wrote on the first anniversary of Mark's death. He said they had yet to escape the cougar, which attacked them in memories, flashbacks, and nightmares.

They have ventured into the woods again. First Dave and Kathy took Rachel on a quarter-mile hike. Rachel was bolder than her mother, Kathy later told her brother. But they came home safe, just as they expected they would on the day Mark died—just as every other family hiking the park that day did.

16

CUYAMACA RANCHO STATE PARK

In most California state parks, cougar reports filed by rangers seem tame: "Lion passing through wildlands" or "A camper reported that she saw a lion across the road" or "lion stood ground and watched people in campsite #4."

But in Cuyamaca Rancho State Park, a cluster of high, cool canyons right behind San Diego, throughout the 1990s the reports read more like a police blotter. Park visitors were "confronted by a lion" or "chased by a lion at close range" or "threatened." A ten-year-old girl was bitten; a three-year-old was rushed; bicyclists were confronted. Up until 1998 Cuyamaca dispatch typically fielded twice the number of cougar complaints as other California state parks.

"Lions at Cuyamaca have been known to be unusually aggressive," says the park's official map. Visitors who wish to protect themselves are encouraged to carry walking sticks, which rangers find leaning against trailhead signs.

You couldn't blame it on one or two bad cats. Between 1987 and 1998 game wardens responding to complaints killed some twenty cougars here. And yet the complaints continued.

Cuyamaca is what the Kumeyaay Indians called this place. It means "the rain beyond." A mile high in the arid Peninsular Range, the park's green glens are unlike anything else in that part of Southern California.

For up to two weeks after a winter storm, the oak and pine forests hold snow, beckoning sunburnt San Diegans. On a clear day you can see the city from the 6,500-foot summit of Cuyamaca Peak. Three miles wide and ten miles long, the park draws roughly a half million people each year.

When then head ranger Laura Itogawa was assigned to Cuyamaca in 1988, she heard a few odd cougar stories but shrugged them off as flukes. One animal had been shot by a Fish and Game lieutenant named Bob Turner after it had holed up in the scout camp's ceremonial tepee. It turned out to have bubonic plague. Other cougars had frightened park visitors, reportedly by following or rushing them. Like her staff, Laura chalked the incidents up to city people intimidated at the sight of a large animal without a leash. Her attitude toward cougars was just like most rangers': Visitors who got to see one were lucky.

Nothing happened during her first five years to change her mind.

Laura had all but grown up in the ranger service. A native of the San Diego suburbs, she turned her love of desert and mountain hiking into a job leading overnight hiking trips. Then she became a seasonal ranger. At nineteen she left college to work full time for California parks.

Laura is five feet one, 110 pounds, fit and forceful, a woman who has spent her career in lug-soled boots and green jeans with a pistol on her hip. But a ranger's gun is for controlling humans, not for killing animals. Or at least that's what she thought those first years at Cuyamaca.

Then in June of 1993 a lion stalked a young family on the Azalea Glen Trail in the heart of the park. The man and his wife had one child in a backpack, the other firmly in hand. The man held a six-foot walking stick before him to fend off the lion. The animal batted at the stick as the family backed all the way to camp. The next day, Bob Turner tracked it down and shot it.

Laura talked over the Azalea Glen incident with her boss, the park superintendent. They agreed to increase the number of warning signs, but it didn't seem like enough. This cougar was more aggressive than any she had heard of. More to the point, it sounded like the cougars in stories she had dismissed when she arrived at Cuyamaca. You could second-guess Bob's decision to kill it, but she had read about serious maulings in British Columbia and couldn't imagine what she'd say to a parent if a child were hurt by an aberrant cougar the park had chosen to tolerate.

Laura met with biologists, wardens, and rangers and then wrote new cougar rules for Cuyamaca. From now on the park would close after worrisome incidents. Bold cats would be killed, particularly those that approached to within a hundred feet of people in broad daylight. Laura didn't like the harsh sound of the new rules any more than her rangers did, but she told herself what she told them: Removal of aggressive cougars would help ensure that the public supported the species as a whole.

That September a lion chased a couple on horseback for more than a quarter mile down the Stonewall Creek firebreak. Spotting a cougar on the trail, the riders had reined in their horses, waiting for it to see them and run away. Instead it turned, stared, and began to pad toward them. Spooked, they galloped away with the cougar in hot pursuit.

This lion had broken all the new rules.

Laura and her boss decided to close the park for two weeks, the biologists' best guess at how long a cougar might hang around if it had a deer carcass cached nearby. She called in the federal hunters from Animal Damage Control (now called Wildlife Services). ADC was an agency of the U.S. Department of Agriculture. Historically, the bulk of its work involved killing predators deemed a burden to farmers and ranchers. But in an increasingly urban world the mission had expanded to include calls like this one.

The federal hunters conducted a thorough but ultimately unsuccessful search for the cat. The fact that no cougar was killed did not keep people from complaining. "Aren't rangers supposed to keep hunters out of the parks?" they asked. Merchants complained that the overly strong park response and resulting negative press had overstated the risk and scared away business. Some park users and local Fish and Game officers, meanwhile, griped that park staff were so focused on wildlife preservation that they hadn't taken confrontations seriously enough. The present situation, they said, was the result.

On reopening day the campers came, but they were jumpy and cat-happy. With a *Los Angeles Times* reporter and photographer tagging along, Laura headed out to check the first report: A camper had seen a cougar crossing a road. En route, her radio hissed to life. A cougar had just sauntered through the 120-person group camp, circling tents and sniffing the backside of a woman bent over tying her shoe. Laura hurried to the group camp and was looking for tracks when the radio spat out words she did not want to hear: A cougar had mauled a dog at the other end of the group camp. Laura gunned her car the quarter mile down the road.

A word like mauled can mean something different to an excited civilian than to a ranger. But there was no mistaking this: The tiny dog was alive, but lying on the ground with its shoulder torn open.

"It went up there," the owner cried, pointing up the nearby fire road.

Laura took several deep breaths as she slid the pole gate out of the way. This cat had to be killed, she realized, and there was no time to call Bob Turner or the federal hunters for help. As a ranger she had shot deer thrashing in ditches after vehicle collisions, but that was mercy. This was going to be different, more like what game wardens did.

She called into the radio, "537? 225." She was rolling quietly up the fire road on a thick mat of pine needles and spongy forest duff, peering into the trees on either side. "225, go ahead," her boss, Greg Picard, came back right away.

"We've got a lion that mauled a dog and they say it's right ahead of me on the road and it's been in the full campground," she told him. "I believe it's a take."

"According to the protocol, I concur," Picard said. "It's a take."

A patch of sunshine twenty-five feet away caught her eye.

"Oop! There he is now!" she told Picard, and signed off. The cougar stood in a little clearing with his ears pricked. He looked playful to her and smaller than she had expected. She heard the reporters pull in behind her, followed by Earl Jones, a ranger who had trained with her in the 1970s and now worked for her.

Out of her vehicle now, she and Earl both jacked shells into their guns and moved slightly apart. They shouldered their shotguns, aimed, and fired. When she refocused after the recoil, the cougar was gone. She looked at Jones. "Where did it go?"

"Up the draw," he said, pointing with his chin.

They climbed. Almost immediately she saw the cougar, lying under a manzanita bush twenty feet away, flicking its tail. "There he is," she called as she leveled her shotgun, fired, and hit.

"He's still alive; shoot him again," she said. Earl did, and the cougar stopped moving.

Relief and regret overwhelmed her. Jones, who stands better than six feet tall and is as fit and slim as Laura, rubbed his temples. The photographer's camera clicked away.

"We need a private moment," Earl said, raising a hand toward the lens. The camera stopped.

"I need a hug," he told Laura and she wrapped her arms around him. When they stepped back, Earl was holding his face in one hand, shotgun in the other, while Laura stood grimacing at the sky. The shutter clicked.

"It's done," she told Picard back at her car. She would later learn that, in the confused moments before the cougar attacked the dog, it had also bitten a little girl. The footprints of the dead cat matched plaster casts of the lion that had chased the riders two weeks before.

The next morning, a photo of Laura and Earl crying over a dead cougar was on the front page of the *Los Angeles Times*. Hate mail and phone calls began pouring in.

"You tell Officer Jones and Officer Itogawa they're going to hell and I'm going to pray for them to go to hell," a caller said.

One cryptic critic pasted the photo from the *Times* onto the lower body of a woman clipped from a pornographic magazine, and mailed it to Laura.

Some park rangers were just as furious about the killing as the callers. Area game wardens disagreed; it had been necessary to kill the cat, but not to cry about it in front of a news photographer. Bob thought the crying part was silly too, but he could relate to Laura's situation. Everyone's a critic when you're making judgment calls about safety and wildlife. He was glad a ranger had finally taken responsibility for some of the park's dirty work.

Laura hunkered down and waited. The critics quieted. So did the cougars.

The next spring, a cougar rushed a three-year-old boy on the Azalea Glen Trail. When the boy's father threatened it with a stick, it initially bared its teeth and crouched low. Then it fled. It was hunted down and killed; so was the next cougar to confront a visitor that year.

Laura believed the biting of the little girl had at least convinced the park's other rangers that bold cats were a serious risk. But there was a big difference between the rangers, still inclined to give cougars every benefit of the doubt, and Bob Turner and the game wardens, who were not. Laura's sympathies were divided.

She was in a meeting with the park's volunteer corps upstairs in the historic stone headquarters on December 10 when a ranger barked her call number over the radio. Two hikers had just shown up with a backpack, a knit cap, a pair of women's glasses—and a tooth. They'd found the items near a puddle of blood on the fire road up on Cuyamaca Peak.

Minutes later one of the hikers, an off-duty California Highway Patrolwoman, handed Laura the blue daypack. It was slimy with what felt like saliva. The rangers Laura had sent to check the scene radioed to say they were on-site and could see something blue off in the bushes.

"Proceed single file with your guns drawn," Laura told them.

"We've got an 11-44," the ranger radioed back a few minutes later. That meant a dead body on the ground. She drove up the steep fire road as fast as she safely could. "What do I want, an ax murderer or a lion?" she asked herself aloud and instantly knew the answer. "An ax murderer."

Laura, her rangers, and a San Diego County deputy walked single-file through the brush. The dead woman's blue sweatpants were bunched at her ankles. She was mostly naked and there were too many puncture wounds in her back to count. But as Laura stared, the picture came into focus. The sweatpants hadn't been yanked down; they were snagged on a tree-limb. The punctures weren't stab wounds. They came in sets of four. Her scalp had been peeled, starting at the nape. No human did this.

The longer she stood over the body, the sadder she became. The woman had been dragged by her head to this dark spot in the woods. But she must have been alive when she got there because her arms were not trailing. They were pulled up to cradle her head. Judging by the smears on the woman's right arm, she had mopped the blood from her forehead before she died. The smears were bright and wet. She had probably been alive fifteen minutes earlier.

The sheriff's deputy was convinced the woman had been murdered. He began hanging crime scene tape. Laura was sure he was wrong. Those were bite wounds; they could only have been the work of a cougar. But the scene couldn't be disturbed until police investigators agreed. Dispatch said the detectives' arrival would depend on how many murders there had been in San Diego that day. She asked dispatch to call Bob Turner. It was 11:30 A.M. This cougar had to die, today if possible.

The two appeared unlikely friends, but that was what they'd finally become. Born of California pioneer stock, like Laura Bob had grown up hiking. But he was also a deer hunter, usually in the foothills north and south of the park. Also like Laura, he had started out as a ranger, patrolling citified parks where scuffles with what he called "human trash" were common. He kept himself fit, wore a thick mustache, and drove a big truck. He also armed himself with a pistol, a steady stream of politically incorrect jokes, and a firm grasp of field biology on which Laura had come to depend.

It was Bob's day off, but when he heard, "They think someone's been killed by a lion," he jumped in his truck and sped the fifteen minutes to the park.

The park rangers could talk all they wanted about how bold cougars are merely curious and should be left alone. And the public could fire off as much hate mail as it pleased. As he swung out of his truck on Cuyamaca Peak, he promised himself: If a cougar had killed this woman, he would find it, and it would die.

But the deputy wouldn't let Bob near the body. Homicide still hadn't arrived with their tweezers and Ziploc baggies. Bob listened to Laura's description of the wounds and thought her assessment was probably correct. But he couldn't be sure until he saw for himself, and he wouldn't turn the hounds loose until he was sure.

"Let me tell you something, people," he told the small crew waiting with him, bundled against a sharp, chill wind. "If this is a lion, the fact that he killed somebody shows that he's not afraid of us. So keep your eyes open and don't be surprised if we see him peeking around a rock or over a log at us."

Laura got more spooked as the daylight began to fade. She still didn't know the victim's name, but having spent the entire afternoon fifteen feet from her, she began to feel as if she knew her. They wore the same cheap Timex outdoor watch. They both had sun wrinkles around their eyes.

Laura would later learn that the victim had been a bird-watcher, like many of Laura's friends. Iris Kenna, fifty-six, had been a guidance counselor at an alternative high school in San Diego. The job gave her plenty of time to load up her Toyota pickup and drive the West Coast or the desert Southwest to go birding.

As Laura waited, she had the strong sense that the cat was out there, just like Bob said.

"You know what. I'm feeling really weird," Laura told the beefy deputy she had assigned to stand guard over the crime scene with her.

"I am, too," the big guy said, looking around.

It was almost dark when the homicide detective finally arrived, straight off the streets of San Diego. He wore an expensive wool overcoat, a suit, and shiny dress shoes. Bob and Laura stopped him on the pavement of the Cuyamaca Peak road.

"I can really help you guys out here if you just let me look at the body," Bob said, explaining who he was and that Laura thought the wounds matched cougar bite marks. The detective let him into the crime scene.

Bob was instantly certain. All over the woman's back and shoulders were sets of four tooth punctures in a characteristic box pattern. The twelve-inch gaping rip under her left arm looked like the work of that huge thumb claw.

The woman had apparently survived the first leaping tackle, even though her head had hit the ground hard enough to knock out a tooth. Bob cringed in sympathy. It's difficult enough to shake a clinging, five-pound housecat loose from your arm if it wants to hurt you. And this was a wildcat more than twenty times heavier, with five big fish hooks on every paw and four big canine teeth in a bone-cracking jaw.

Iris's body was bagged for removal, and Bob moved in. A houndsman's radio dog collar was strapped to a nearby sapling. The removable magnetic "on" switch was tied to a deer Bob had shot to fool the cougar when it returned. If the deer moved, the radio collar would sound.

Back down the mountain, Turner and a small group of federal

hunters and wardens packed their gear and checked guns and flashlights. They were speculating how long they would need to wait when one of the federal hunters realized he hadn't turned on the receiver yet. When he did, the radio collar was already sounding. It had been no more than twenty minutes since they left the scene.

Back on Cuyamaca Peak, they found the deer carcass gone. There were no drag marks. This lion was big enough to pick up a deer like a sack of groceries and carry her away.

The hounds were barking from the back of the truck like they'd already struck scent. Released, they headed south, baying the distinctive bark that says the scent is fresh. The lion and dogs contoured along the ridge for a half mile before the lion treed. When Bob arrived, he trained his flashlight upward.

All of the problem cougars he'd seen in Cuyamaca were juveniles, sixty-, seventy-, and eighty-pounders. He thought of them as troubled teenagers. This was a big male, 130 pounds from the look of him.

Laura didn't sleep well that night. Her mind was still up on Cuyamaca Peak. In the morning she ducked into the park's maintenance shop to look at the dead cougar Bob and his hunters had brought in.

"Look what you've done," she silently chided the body before her. Hunting advocates would use this as evidence that recreational cougar hunting must be resumed in California. "Look what you've done to your friends."

In the years after Iris's death, her birdwatcher friends would criticize the killing, saying that the cougar was only behaving naturally and that Iris would have wanted to die as she had, getting woven back into the web of life as food for a wild animal.

Easy to say when you didn't see the wounds, reply both Laura and Bob. They snort at the idea that anybody would choose the lonely agony so obvious to them that day on Cuyamaca Peak.

For a year after Iris's death, there were no serious cougar problems. Then in January of 1996, a woman had to charge her horse at a cougar that confronted her. Bob shot it the next day when it charged another game warden. Laura began to think there was some genetic quirk in the park's cats that made them more aggressive.

In September 1998 Bob and another warden killed four Cuyamaca cougars in two days, all near the same horse camp, after campers reported a series of stalkings and mock charges. Shawn Pirtle was the first game warden on the scene. He was amazed when a park ranger suggested that he shoot only if, when they found the culprits, the animals failed to run away from them as well. He was more amazed when, after what seemed to him four such necessary removals, the same old disagreements blew up in letters to the editor and angry mail to park headquarters and the local California Fish and Game office.

Even though those four cats were probably siblings, Bob was convinced it wasn't genetics so much as environment that made some Cuyamaca cougars dangerous. He dealt with cougars all over San Diego County but only saw cats that aggressively confronted humans in Cuyamaca, where a steady stream of people flooded the lion's habitat. Cats that see people from their first day out of the womb are more likely to experiment with them as a possible food source, he said.

For most of her life, Laura had thought nothing of backpacking alone in the Sierra Nevada Mountains and the deserts of Arizona, sharing terrain with both cougars and bears. But she stopped walking her own park's trails alone. To this day she won't make her rangers do it. In fact, she tries to discourage them. The park's cougars aren't the only reason, but they're the most significant.

On the rare occasions that Laura does have to move through the park's backcountry alone, she carries a heavy stick slung across her shoulders to protect her neck. She has picked up the habit of spinning about often, keeping track of what's behind her.

In 1999 the state of California decided to take a hard look at the Cuyamaca cougar question. The legislature approved two hundred thousand dollars for a study of cougar-human interactions in the park. Within a year that money had attracted additional funding and the scope of the project grew. Called the Southern California Cougar Project, it would be a ten-year study of mountain lions, humans, mule deer, and desert bighorn sheep. Researchers Linda Sweanor and Kenny Logan were hired to lead the lion portion of the study.

There were no strange reports of overly bold cougars in 1999.

There were none in 2000. The whole thing seemed to have stopped, just like that. Laura was surprised at how fast the disconcerting reports of the 1990s began to fade from her rangers' memories, almost as though they'd never happened.

Ken and Linda had just moved into a little house on park grounds in early 2001 when Laura and her husband found a road-killed deer. They knew the researchers needed bait, so they brought the 150-pound carcass to the little house. Ken put it into the bed of his pickup truck for the night. The next morning it was gone. A light dusting of snow on the ground recorded the incident: A full-grown male cougar had hopped into Ken's truck and taken the carcass. It was found about a hundred yards away in heavy brush. There were no drag marks: It had been carried there.

Laura remembers that Ken was startled. She wasn't.

"Welcome to Cuyamaca," she said. "This is how our cats behave."

That cougar became M-1, the first male radio collared for the study.

But as the summer of 2001 also drew to a close with no reports of aggressive cougar behavior to hand to the researchers, Laura was almost annoyed. Here were top-notch scientists ready to observe and try to understand the phenomenon but there was no phenomenon to observe.

One of the study's attempts to learn how park cougars behaved toward human visitors involved first measuring human use of selected park trails. The researchers then analyzed that data against the locations of their collared cats. They found that cougars utilized those trails just as they did the land around busy campgrounds or park buildings, but they did not use them during hours of high human use. They were most likely to visit high-use areas at night. It appeared that Cuyamaca's cougars were actively avoiding human contact.

This was particularly striking in light of the effort cougars had to expend to do so. For every square kilometer of park, there are two kilometers of trail. And yet Linda Sweanor was receiving only about twenty cougar sighting reports a year, many of them questionable.

Up to this time studies of cougar-human interaction tended to rely on sighting reports. The first problem with sightings as data is that they, by necessity, tell only one side of the story. The witness can't say what the cougar was doing before it was spotted or after it left. Nor can a person tell about the cougar that was there but not seen. The second problem with sightings is that they're notoriously difficult to validate. Sometimes they're flat strange.

One report Linda fielded in Cuyamaca involved a man who said he was sitting in his tent with a hand against its interior wall when he felt pressure against his palm. An animal he decided must be a cougar had just lain down out there, tucked up against his tent. And then, he said, it began to purr. The man was enchanted. He and the lion had shared an emotional experience, he told Linda.

Ken went to the campground to investigate. Outside the tent he found a set of very fresh raccoon tracks.

The researchers released a report in 2003. State wildlife experts had estimated that the hullabaloo of the 1990s was caused, at any one time, by perhaps a dozen cougars whose home ranges included the park. It turned out that the number was smaller, five or six, and that on a given day only one or two of those animals might actually be in the 25,000-acre park.

The Cuyamaca cougars lived closely alongside park users and area residents. Seventy-three percent of prey cache sites were within three hundred meters of a trail or fire road. Of twenty study animals, seven were found to occasionally prey on domestic animals outside the park. All territorial adults included significant chunks of private property in their territories. And although four were shot for attacking or threatening domestic animals, for the most part these animals conducted their lives side by side with humans, unseen, which was exactly like nearly everywhere else cougars and humans coexist, and nothing like the park in the 1990s.

The Southern California Cougar Study continues, but Linda and Ken are gone. They left shortly before the largest fire in the state's history ripped through Cuyamaca. The Cedar Fire burned 99 percent of the park. The deer left for lack of forage. The cougars left for lack of deer and cover. It was 2005 before the entire park finally reopened and park visitation returned to prefire levels. By then the deer were long back. So were the cougars.

According to biologist Mike Puzzo, who currently works on the study, its driving question no longer concerns cougar-human interactions. The researchers study how mountain lions utilize developed and fragmented areas. Ten cougars currently wear collars for the study. The researchers are actively working to collar more, but none has been captured in the park since Linda and Ken left. At least two adult cougars known to use the park are uncollared.

Meanwhile Bob Turner has retired and Laura Itogawa, now superintendent, is preparing to as well. According to Laura and her supervising ranger, Bob Hillis, the park's cougar-human pattern may again be changing. Twice in 2005 and twice by July of 2006 park visitors reported seeing cougars in broad daylight in areas of high human use, exactly the behavior Linda and Ken had *not* found in their study animals. These cougars stared at the people without approaching, but also without reticence. In each case the humans retreated and were not followed.

17

LUCY OBERLIN, 1997

"Why are you getting out of the car?" Diane asked nervously.

"I want to see if I can stand," said Lucy Oberlin. Ahead of them, a uniformed park employee bent into the window of a car, talking tourists through a Cuyamaca Rancho State Park map. Lucy found herself waiting politely until the employee glanced back.

"I want to report a mountain lion attack," she said, startled by how hoarse she sounded.

"Oh, did you just see one, dear?"

"No, we just had a twenty-minute fight with one."

The woman stared for a moment before replying, "Well, you don't look injured."

"I want to make a report," croaked Lucy stubbornly.

The woman looked more closely, and then her voice became briskly professional. "Let me call a ranger to talk to you, OK?"

Lucy and Diane told their story to the heavy-set ranger who arrived a few minutes later. He took careful notes, but he also said things that made Lucy uncomfortable. He suggested they not repeat their story to the media. He told them park rangers receive death threats every time "one of these things happens." He joked that the lion exhibited good taste in singling out these two women. He seemed to think they were overreacting, that they might make people think mountain lions were dangerous.

"But they *are* dangerous," Lucy thought. This was 1997, and it was common knowledge that weird cougar encounters occurred in this park. A woman had been killed a few years back, a child bitten. And today she or Diane might have died. Something should be done. She wasn't thinking well enough yet to have an idea what, but clearly this man in front of her was one of the people that ought to do it.

Lucy had run the trails in Cuyamaca for seventeen years. When she lived in San Diego, she made the hour-long drive once a week. For the last five years she'd lived only a few minutes from the park on Interstate 8, in a little town called Alpine. This allowed her to run and walk Cuyamaca's oak-forested hills nearly every other day.

Often she ran with Diane Shields, her partner in a cookie dough company called "Your Mama's Cookies." Lucy was forty. Her passion for running weathered her skin brown between the freckles. Her hair was dyed blonde, then sunbleached to an uncompromising near white. Lucy and Diane had been friends for nearly two decades.

Lucy talks in emotional hyperbole. If she was frightened, she describes queasy, knee-quivering terror. If she was sad, she bawled for an hour, couldn't eat, couldn't sleep. But you get the impression, studying her ramrod carriage and direct gaze, that she's never met a problem too big, after the emoting, to beat.

On this baking August day in 1997, the two had taken Lucy's gray minivan to Cuyamaca's Cold Stream Trailhead. Their route would provide a pretty view from the summit of Stonewall Peak and a fourteen-mile out-and-back run. At about 1 P.M., they strapped on fanny packs and water bottles. Each grabbed a slim black canister of pepper spray.

The women had started carrying pepper spray years before after encountering perhaps thirty armed men on a Cuyamaca trail. The men had broken out in excited yells and begun chasing them. When the women gained a little distance, they ducked into thick brush. The men ran past, yelling, "chicas," and "andele," and other words the runners didn't understand. Encounters with what locals call "illegals" are not uncommon in Cuyamaca and surrounding areas. The border is barely a day's determined walk south.

These days, the incident grown vague in their minds, the two carried the canisters mostly from habit. They ran north on Cold Stream Trail, Lucy leading. They intersected the Stonewall Peak Trail, which took them to the top of the mountain. From the summit the women could see desert stretching away from the mountains upon which they stood, like ocean from an island. On a clear day they would have glimpsed the Pacific, but haze to the west blocked that thin blue line. The women ran another half hour past the peak before turning back. About a mile before Cold Stream Trail would deliver them to the van, they began walking to cool down. Diane was talking excitedly to Lucy's back about something important that neither would later recall. Then Lucy saw the mountain lion.

It stood in the trail about thirty feet away. It stared at the women. Cuyamaca's aggressive lions had gotten a lot of press, so Lucy's response was fast and smart.

"Diane, there's a mountain lion. Start screaming!"

"What, what?" Diane replied lightly.

"Diane! Mountain lion. Start screaming!"

As though spurred by Lucy's yell, the lion began trotting toward them. The movement drew Diane's eyes. Now she got it. Both women screamed hard and waved their arms. The lion neither slowed nor hastened. Lucy extended the pepper spray before her. This was not supposed to happen. They were supposed to yell and stand their ground and act big, and the animal would stop. But it wasn't stopping.

Frantic, she punched the button. A thin brown aerosol line of fluid, about as wide as a pencil lead, sprayed out from the little canister. The spray only reached about six feet before dispersing—several feet short of the lion.

The big animal stopped, pulled its head back, and sniffed. Then, its eyes never leaving the women, it backed up the embankment left of the trail and dropped into a half-crouch.

Lucy felt naked in the middle of the trail. A nearby cluster of five or six slim-trunked trees laced with brush offered at least the illusion of protection. Still yelling, she drew Diane up the slope, and the two pressed close to the trees.

Lucy felt something bang against her left arm. "Take it," Diane yelled. Lucy's free hand closed around a five-foot-long stick.

The lion came then, fast and low. Lucy thrashed the brush with her stick. Diane threw rocks. The cat stopped just out of spray range, then backed up, eyes still on the women. "I'm covering you. Pick up more rocks," Lucy ordered.

"I'm scared. I can't."

"You have to. I'm covering you. Please, you have to."

Diane bent to the ground.

And so it went, for what Lucy would later guess was fifteen minutes. The lion would stare, silent and intent, muscles bunched beneath the tan hide. Then it would drop low and rush them with ground-hugging grace. The women yelled at the lion to leave them alone, yelled for help. When they had something to say to each other, they yelled it. They banged their sticks and threw the rocks that Diane found at her feet. Despite all their noise, the lion came a little closer each time before it stopped. As it retreated, its ears would rise to the sulky, dangerous half-mast position every housecat owner knows. Then the ears would again slick down to the round skull and it would charge toward the yelling, stick-banging women. Then it would withdraw again, rush, withdraw.

Lucy was sure she and Diane would escape—she would kill the lion if she had to—but when she tried to imagine how, her imagination painted pictures in blood. With each image, she became more terrified. "This is really going to hurt," she thought.

The standoff was taking a greater toll on Diane. At one point she screamed, "This has got to stop! We've got to get out of here."

"We can't run, Diane. We have to get out of here alive."

Moments later, she glanced back to see Diane rocking rhythmically forward and back, white-faced, eyes half-lidded and vague. Lucy grabbed her arm, squeezed as hard as she could and yelled in her face, "Stay with me! You've got to stay with me."

Once more the lion rushed in, but this time it didn't stop. When it reached the far side of their little thicket, Lucy frantically thumbed her pepper spray, discharging the last of the thin stream directly onto the left side of the cat's head and neck. Bull's-eye! The cat reared violently away, front paws scrubbing at the air, almost toppling over backward.

This time Lucy imagined for a moment that it was leaving, but it only retreated a little further from the trail. It climbed onto a low boulder and crouched, still staring.

The women were hoarse from shouting and lightheaded from fear. Neither doubted that they were fighting for their lives; neither believed, as they had at first, that the cat might tire of these noisy, rock-throwing creatures and simply leave. Diane, pale and shaking, held the precious final canister of pepper spray.

Something had to change. Lucy eyeballed a heavy-trunked tree four feet from their current, precarious refuge, four feet closer to the parking lot and the van.

The first few times they tried for it, the lion dropped from its boulder and rushed. Its rushes were only feints of a few yards now, but they drove the women back. On the seventh try, the lion allowed them to reach the tree. So they picked another tree. The animal didn't move as they slipped across the gap. They picked a third.

Six trees later, they reached a bend in the trail. From here it was a straight shot to the road, still nearly a mile away.

Lucy and Diane hesitated, then slipped around the corner. The two began walking quickly, shoulder to shoulder and sometimes back to back, eyes straining into the heavy scrub oak and manzanita. Was the cat still on its boulder behind them or was it already ahead, crouched in the underbrush beside the trail?

When they could see the highway paralleling the trail through the trees, they cut through a steep gully to intersect it. They walked down the middle of the road the quarter mile to Lucy's car. Lucy dropped her stick at the car door, but she had to help Diane pry cramped fingers from around hers, revealing bloody half-moons on her palm. They got into the van and, feeling the silliness of it, each reached out to lock her door.

Lucy's voice rasped in her throat for two months. She believes she is alive because neither woman panicked and fled, because that particular day they had been running together, and because they habitually carried pepper spray.

Although she's pretty sure the first rangers she spoke with didn't take her story seriously, her report was one of several that led to the killing of four aggressive Cuyamaca lions. If she thought that was the end of it, though, she was wrong. When they read about the dead lions in the paper, Lucy's friends told her she shouldn't have reported the incident.

"I believe he would have killed someone," she told them, but her friends seemed not to hear. They talked about how beautiful lions are, how naturally curious—like house cats at play. They assured her confidently that the lion had never intended her harm.

Others were less kind. The park is known cougar habitat, they said. Strange cougar stories were common, so it wasn't like Lucy didn't know the risk. Yet she and Diane ran there anyway. The encounter was the women's fault but it was cougars that had paid the price, as usual.

One day weeks after the encounter and subsequent killings, a stranger marched up to Lucy in the grocery store. "You're the woman who killed four mountain lions, aren't you? You did kill them, you know."

The criticism made her cry, but it didn't stop her from running. Her solution? She purchased a .380 to carry in her fanny pack.

Guns are illegal in Cuyamaca Rancho State Park. That and Lucy's hippy upbringing in mellow Carmel, California, made her uneasy about the lethal weight of the thing against her body. But she couldn't imagine not running. She felt those hours on Cuyamaca's forested trails made her a better, stronger person. She also couldn't imagine running without more serious protection than a finger-sized can of pepper spray. She wore a seatbelt when she drove a car, and she would now carry a gun in lion country.

This was not the hysterical victim who had expected the rangers to do "something." Perhaps she had internalized some of the criticism of those first, tearful weeks after the encounter. Lucy still believed that running in the park was her right, but maybe that right had to be earned. Not by killing—she didn't ever expect to actually pull the little gun's trigger—but by being able to defend herself. Being ready.

For nearly a year the women avoided the area around Cold Stream Trail with superstitious distaste. Then one warm afternoon the next April, as they trained for a thirty-eight-mile race to be held that fall in Yosemite National Park, they decided to run the Eastside Trail, an old favorite of theirs. It would cross Cold Stream Trail about seven miles into their run.

Early on as they forded the Sweetwater River, they passed the outside edge of Cuyamaca Outdoor School, to which many San Diego County schools send their sixth-graders. The women saw a dozen kids, sweatshirts knotted about their waists, teetering across the shallow river on boulders and logs. A single adult walked several yards ahead. Two kids straggled ten yards behind. The empty air between those two and the rest made Lucy nervous. She promised herself that when her two young kids went to the school, she'd go too. And on hikes she'd bring up the rear.

Lucy no longer believed she could have killed, barehanded, the cat that had charged her and Diane. A game warden named Bob Turner had shown her police photos of two women killed by mountain lions. The victims' devastating wounds stole her illusions. The lion had been in control that day on Cold Stream Trail. Lucy and Diane left unharmed because it let them leave. By what margin, for what reason, she would never know. She thought about the gun, stored that day in Diane's fanny pack, and as usual she felt steadier.

As they began their return, the women again crossed the Sweetwater River, here only a narrow trickle, and stopped on a cool, damp sandbar to stretch. They decided they felt more comfortable returning to Cold Stream Trail than they had expected to. They reminded each other how slim were the odds, even in strange Cuyamaca, that they'd ever again face a mountain lion.

On the way down, a soft carpet of pine needles made running pleasant. Soon they were back at the camp, which this time they passed directly through. At the river bench about fifty kids played tetherball, volleyball, badminton, and basketball. No adults were in sight. Then a bell rang from the camp buildings above. Half of the kids broke away and headed uphill. They must eat in shifts, Lucy thought. All the adults must be up there making dinner happen.

The women dropped to the little river, crossed on the same logs and rocks they'd seen the youthful hikers use, and zigzagged up a sandy trail on the far side. The trail hugged the lip of the steep bank, fifteen feet above the water. The Sweetwater River here ran knee-deep and quiet over rocks and strips of sand. The far bank rose steeply as well.

Again, Lucy saw the lion first. It was across the river, thank God, on the far bank. An utterly irrational thought slipped into her head: If I don't look, it'll go away, or never have been there, or turn into a deer.

She turned her eyes resolutely to the trail ahead. Seconds passed—fifteen, twenty, thirty. Then she couldn't stand it. Her eyes darted left. The lion had not, of course, turned into a deer. It now glided parallel to the women, matching their speed, its body pointed downriver, its small head swiveled toward them, its gaze solid as twin rods.

"Diane? Get out the gun."

The animal was lovely, with a pale face, creamy, soft-looking fur and a long, thick tail it carried high. It seemed much larger than the other one. But although huge and heavy, the animal moved with a weightless grace that made Lucy feel clumsy. It seemed to float above the ground. Tall grasses brushed its belly.

Less than a quarter mile beyond the river, Lucy could see busy Highway 79 through the trees. Diane couldn't fire even if she wanted to. Who knew how far a bad shot might travel? Besides, this cougar was only shadowing them. Did that mean it would attack? Did that mean it wouldn't? Lucy found herself thinking nothing could stare as hard as a lion.

"Take it, take the gun. I can't get a bullet in the chamber."

Diane's tremulous voice alarmed Lucy. She looked back to see her friend extending the gun, barrel down, with a violently shaking arm. An instant later, Diane stumbled to the ground. Lucy caught the gun by reflex. And by reflex her eyes shot to the cougar. It had sunk into a crouch. Suddenly all that was visible were its face and wide, intent eyes. This was not good. This was too much like a year ago. She yanked her friend to her feet. As soon as the women were walking again, the lion also rose and resumed its gliding accompaniment. Détente.

Lucy worked the slide and heard a cartridge click into the chamber. The .380 was ready to fire.

"Don't shoot," Diane said. "There's cars out there."

"I won't. Not unless he comes to the river."

How fast could a mountain lion cross a narrow ribbon of shallow water and fifteen feet of shore? Before she could shoot twice? Once? Lucy had never practiced on a moving target. She felt queasy.

For more than a mile the lion shadowed the women. Lucy became more and more certain that it would not turn and charge, but she couldn't relax.

They caught their last glimpse of the lion when the trail curved away from the river into heavy brush. It was still staring, but it made no move to follow. Two minutes later they turned the last corner before the parking area and saw a young couple strolling ahead of them. The woman wore a white tube top and clear, platform jellies. She was tiny, the bones in her shoulders and arms readily visible beneath pale skin. They looked like city folk, a distinction locals were quick to make once they themselves no longer were.

"Are you headed to your car?" called Lucy.

"Why?" chirped the woman.

"*Because*," said Lucy, mimicking the woman's tone. "We've been followed by a mountain lion for the past mile."

"Oh goody," said the woman. "I'd love to see a mountain lion. Let's go look for it. Where did you see it? When?"

"Unless you're carrying a gun or pepper spray, I don't think you want to do that." Lucy allowed her face to harden with disgust. She still clutched the .380, although she tried to conceal it against her body.

The man looked at Lucy and back at his companion. Lucy thought perhaps he had seen the gun. "No. We're headed to our car," he said quickly.

Lucy and Diane brushed past them into the parking lot. Her stomach felt full of something. Fear? Relief? Whatever it was, she heaved it up onto the ground behind the bumper without embarrassment. Several minutes passed before she was willing to unload the .380 and put it in the trunk. Without it, the short walk to the driver's door stripped her naked.

"I'm sorry. I can't drive yet," she mumbled, beginning to be ashamed. Don't look and it'll disappear? How stupid.

"It was a beautiful lion," said Diane. As usual, once the crisis was past, she was rock steady. Lucy, who'd felt solid when the moments had been strung together like a tight wire over empty space, now thought she might shake to pieces.

"Beautiful? How can you say that?" she snapped.

"Lucy, it didn't get us. We're OK."

Lucy took a deep breath. Diane was right. "We're OK," she agreed.

And she remembered that she had also thought the animal beautiful.

Nevertheless, she called in a report that night. Over the next few days, several park staffers walked her through the encounter. Most seemed unsympathetic, even doubtful. One woman Lucy took to be a ranger said that she herself had once viewed a lion and kitten and found it a lovely sight. When the woman added that she'd been sitting in a car at the time, Lucy was disgusted.

One ranger, a woman named Laura Itogawa, sounded more sympathetic. She asked Lucy to understand that the park stood in an awkward place, sworn to protect its wild inhabitants as well as its human visitors. This ranger assured Lucy that the cougar she described was not behaving in a way the park considered normal or safe, and that park staff did, indeed, have concerns about Cuyamaca's lions.

Lucy called Fish and Game's Bob Turner, unsure what she wanted, perhaps just someone to take her seriously. Bob suggested the cat might have been using the women to hunt, watching to see if they would flush deer. Lucy didn't buy it. She thought Bob was trying to make her feel better by making the lion's behavior seem less threatening. It wasn't so strange to her that a lion might let humans flush prey, but with its camouflage coloring and boneless grace, it could have stayed out of sight if it wished. Instead, it had allowed them to know it was matching them, step for step. Why?

Lucy still runs in Cuyamaca Rancho State Park, but she no longer allows her children to hike there. After the second incident, she seriously considered quitting trail running. But if she had spent the last twenty years running on city streets, she decided, more bad things would have happened and she wouldn't have stood atop nearly so many mountains. She told herself that while she could say that she had had two frightening lion encounters in a year, she could also say that she'd only had two in twenty years.

But Lucy now thinks that she will meet a lion again, that Cuyamaca Rancho's lions look at people with the same predatory speculation with which they survey deer. When she confronts the next lion, she's decided, she will live. If necessary, the cat will die.

18
RON RECEVEUR, 1997

Ron Receveur's short, powerful build bespeaks a man who works hard. He holds his muscular arms slightly bent, as though at any moment he might encounter a heavy load that wants carrying. A workingman's tan turns his blue eyes to calm ocean water.

Ron lives in Port Alberni, British Columbia, population 20,000, near Vancouver Island's west coast. Port Alberni calls itself "The Town with a Heart." It was once a fishing and logging boomtown. Now times are harder, but people aren't complaining much. They like living here.

The town is divided by four creeks running west out of the mountains, each creek densely wooded and deeply gullied, each with its own trail system and teenager hideaways. Each funnels wildlife right into the town's picturesque center. Kitsuksis Creek marks the north edge of town. Rogers, Dry, and Shipp Creeks run through the middle.

Partly because of those creeks—habitat highways through town—it seems every Port Albernian has a strange animal encounter story. Unreported to authorities but passed about like spare change, they color the zeitgeist of the town.

In 1992 a cougar nabbed a little dog right downtown and carried it up a tree. Amazingly, the dog survived its journey. Ron Receveur once saw two cougars walking down Shipp Creek Road about a half block from the street's first houses. Not surprisingly, black bears are seen more often than cougars. According to official estimates, there are nearly ten times as many bears as cougars on Vancouver Island.

During 1998's fall salmon feast, hundreds of partygoers wandered toward the festival grounds up one side of a finger-shaped inlet. On the far side a black bear also wandered, searching for fish entrails from the cleaning stations upstream. Only the tourists stopped to stare.

Residents don't mind the bears. The island has never had a serious bear attack. But Port Albernians don't like cougars. They say lions are unpredictable in ways bears are not. They say lions intend harm as bears do not.

Local concern about cougars may explain why, when a mentally disabled man named Lloyd Dayton was found facedown in Kitsuksis Creek one hot July afternoon in 1995, blame fell on a cougar. Port Alberni already had one unexplained murder in its past, a local child whose abduction had almost certainly been the work of a resident. Nobody wanted another.

Still, some officials were certain Lloyd Dayton's killer was no cougar. He had been found floating in a shallow pool, not buried in debris. He had a scattering of pencil-thick punctures on his neck but no obvious claw or bite marks. His brand-new red bike helmet, proudly shown off to friends earlier that day, was still strapped to his head, not a scratch on it.

If Lloyd Dayton had indeed been killed by a cougar, however, he was the first person in recorded history attacked within a town of substantial size. Hunters with trained hounds searched for weeks. Residents were encouraged to call in every cougar sighting. The *Port Alberni Valley Times* repeatedly warned people about cougars and other in-town wildlife.

Eighteen months passed. Then the newspaper exploded in outrage. It had just learned that the killing was being investigated as a homicide and probably had been for months. Suddenly Lloyd Dayton was no longer the island's fourth cougar death in less than twenty years but little Port Alberni's second unexplained murder.

The town had spent those months waiting for a killer cougar to strike again, forbidding its children from playing in the creeks, peering through kitchen windows before taking out the trash on dark nights.

During those nervous months, an even stronger distrust of cougars had developed. The belated truth, that Port Alberni's most dangerous predators were human, wasn't likely to make it go away.

Since then, cougar phobia hasn't faded. Stories like Ron Receveur's keep it alive.

Lloyd Dayton had been dead more than two years on the October morning when Ron decided to try a favorite mushrooming spot on the lower slopes of Mount Arrowsmith, just outside of town. It was pine mushroom season, and this was a good year for pines. Ron had been finding an unusual amount of big number ones, their caps still closed into spheres and worth top dollar. On this day, Ron knew, buyers would be paying twelve dollars a pound for number ones. With a little luck, he would make hundreds of dollars by sundown.

Ron's long-time canine companion, Maggie, had an appointment at the vet, so Ron decided to take her goofy son, Buck, for company. Buck looks a bit like his slim, alert border collie mom, with his glossy black coat and white-splashed chest. He moves dodgy too, like a cow dog. But his Labrador retriever father gave him a bigger frame—Buck weighs seventy-five pounds—and a Lab's gentle eyes.

"He's the fastest Lab I ever had," Ron likes to say. "But he's dumber than a bag of hammers."

That morning Ron tossed his caulked boots into the van. Designed for loggers who work on steep terrain, they have steel "corks" spiked into heavy soles. He pulled on his surveyor's vest. Its pockets contained a water bottle, a small first-aid kit, a wood chisel, and a hunting knife.

Ron had been picking for twenty years, since long before mushrooming became a staple for the townspeople. Now in late summer and fall, when first the chanterelles and then the pine mushrooms pop up, commercial mushroom buyers journeyed to Port Alberni to set up their scales, and locals headed into the mountains to make the easiest money they'd come by all year. Old hand that he was, Ron tried to get there first.

A short drive through quiet morning streets and Ron and Buck were out of the van, trudging straight up Mount Arrowsmith. The slope was so steep Ron felt like he was climbing stairs. Logged years before, it now consisted of thirty-foot-tall, second-growth Douglas firs laced together by shiny-leafed silal, scratchy wild rose, slim maple, willow, and alder. Branches slapped Ron's face and snapped against the two nested five-gallon buckets he hoped to fill with mushrooms. Ron could hear Buck zigzagging through the underbrush nearby, but seldom saw him among the leafy tangle. The dog seemed to be staying closer than usual, perhaps thirty feet off. Ron wondered if the young animal felt insecure without Maggie to buddy with.

The break into what Ron calls "timber" was sudden and sweet. This part of the mountain had never been logged. Here the trees were wide-spaced old giants, with rich loam at their feet and a feeling of weighty peace, as among the stone pillars of a cathedral. This unlogged refuge was where the pine mushrooms grew.

Ron began the mushroom hunter's methodical, zigzagging search up the steep mountainside. He focused on the ground near his feet, training his eyes to the infrequent sight of brown-scaled white caps. Ron was vaguely aware that Buck was still running about in that goofy, oblivious way of his, nose locked to the ground, but still close. Mostly though, Ron hunted.

Slowly his bucket filled as he found first one sparse patch and then another. Bruised mushrooms aren't worth much, so he pried each stem gently from the ground with his chisel. With the first bucket full, Ron unstacked the second. Now when he stopped to pick, he placed the full bucket against his leg so it wouldn't spill its contents down the steep slope.

Then Ron hit a bonanza, a picker's dream. He was in an area where the venerable trees were forty feet apart. A few rotting logs littered the ground. Otherwise it was mossy and bare—except for the pine mushrooms, which suddenly seemed to be everywhere. Ron found a shallow depression where he could safely leave the full bucket and began happily topping the second.

He was nearly finished when he noticed something odd. A log, three feet wide and sixty feet long, was propped over a shallow draw just uphill. This log had legs. Four big, thick legs.

Fanatic that he is, Ron's first disappointed thought was that another picker had stumbled upon this rare wealth of mushrooms, and he was seeing the person's dog. That thought was almost instantly shoved aside by the size of those legs. They were too powerful-looking. They could belong to nothing but a cougar.

Oh shit, he thought. Ron was from Port Alberni, so he didn't feel awe, or wish for a camera, or thank his stars for a sighting as rare as the mushroom patch in which he stood. Instead, his head filled with all the things he'd heard a person was supposed to do to keep from getting hurt: Get big, get loud, don't run away.

A second passed. Then the cat's head appeared where its legs had been. Its eyes were on Buck. The dog stopped his sniffing explorations and turned to Ron as though asking a question.

Then Buck's eyes followed Ron's to the cat, and he began to whine. It felt to Ron like a warning. All hell was about to break loose. Figuring he'd make his move first, Ron began whacking his bucket with the chisel. An instant later, the cougar slipped underneath the log, fast and smooth as though skating on its belly. It was headed straight for Buck. Buck ran too, straight for Ron, whimpering.

If Buck stopped when he got to Ron, Ron figured he'd be the one in trouble. But if Buck kept running, he'd be a dead dog. Which would it be?

The young dog passed three feet to Ron's right. The cougar glided by too, not more than a body length behind the dog. Ron could have touched the tawny animal, but it seemed to see only Buck. The scene was made even more surreal by the fact that neither animal ran full-out: The goofy dog's tail was up like a flag, as though they were playing a game of tag, and the cougar's easy lope seemed designed to maintain the distance, not close it. Maybe it didn't know what to do with a dog that didn't understand he was about to die.

See ya, Buck, Ron thought sadly. How would he tell his wife?

Not because he feared for himself—the cougar wanted Buck, not him—but because his body was buzzing with adrenaline, Ron flung himself downhill, away from what was about to happen to Buck. Half-sliding down the slope, he grabbed his other bucket by its metal bale as he ran past. Now he had fifteen pounds of mushrooms hanging from each arm.

For several minutes, Ron descended through forest stillness. Then the silence was broken by the click of rock on rock, right behind him. His mind supplied an image: the cougar frozen in midleap, aimed like an arrow at the back of his head. He spun, heart in his throat. But it was Buck that ran at him, tongue hanging, tail wagging.

Right behind him was the cougar.

Ron lifted both buckets over his head, yelling wildly. The cat slowed and began circling. Ron set the buckets against his legs, grabbed a couple of rocks, and threw. He missed. The cougar's eyes never left the dog at Ron's feet, but its circling trajectory widened.

The cat was seventy-five feet away when it entered a jumble of windfall. Instantly it became a shadow among shadows. Ron could still make out its long, graceful shape, but if he hadn't known it was there his gaze would have passed over it.

Buck remained pressed against his leg. Ron was glad, because he was pretty sure the dog was safe as long as he stayed close. Now that Buck had somehow made it back unharmed, the man was determined not to give the cougar a second chance. He would get Buck out of there.

Ron began feeling his way once more downhill, this time more cautiously. He kept his eyes on the cat. Something in the animal's stare made him not want to stumble. Nearly crouched, his hand brushed the ground, touched something soft and smooth. The action was reflex: He picked the pine. He felt another, picked it. The third broke in his hand, rendering it unsellable.

This is crazy, he thought. Perhaps that was when Ron realized it was no longer Buck that the cougar's eyes followed. Ron was standing around picking mushrooms while a cougar toyed with him.

So began the pair's second escape. They rushed, slipping and stumbling, down the slope. The dog stayed close by Ron's leg. The cat glided easily down the mountain, beside and just a little behind them.

After a few minutes Ron lost sight of the cougar. He didn't believe it was gone, though. Every dozen steps or so, he began spinning around and lifting the buckets over his head so as to appear big and intimidating. Each time he was half-convinced he would catch the cougar in midleap. Each time he saw nothing but forest shadows.

By now he had his hunting knife in one hand and the chisel in the other, in addition to the bucket bales. If the lion attacked, he would drop the buckets and stab it with both tools. He also thought about slamming a bucket over the cat's head as it sprang, but he rejected that plan because he couldn't make himself dump all those fine, plump number ones.

He kept up a constant yelling as they fled, even after he began to think the cougar might have moved on. Because he needed something to say, he addressed Buck: "Buck, I can't believe you're here. I can't believe you made it. We gotta get out of here, Buck."

Then he'd spin around, buckets raised—just in case.

They reached the road, and a few minutes later the van, without seeing the cougar again. Ron unlocked the back door. Buck jumped in and Ron, instead of walking around to the driver's side, crawled in behind. Sighing with relief, he slammed the door. His legs were rubbery. He decided he'd just sit there for a minute.

"Man, I can't believe you got away," he told his now unconcerned dog.

Ron's breathing had just slowed when movement caught his eye. He peered out the van's back window. It was the cougar.

It was sauntering down the dirt road toward the vehicle. Gone was the intensity of posture and stare. The big animal now looked like an improbably large house cat out for a stroll. It meandered to a stop five feet from the van. It sat.

Its gaze wandered here and there. Its front paws were tucked neatly together. It didn't seem aware that Ron and Buck were so close, literally an arm's reach away, but that closeness hypnotized Ron. He stared, unbelieving, through the dusty window.

But he couldn't stare forever, not even at a cougar that had chased him off the mountain, so after several minutes he moved up to the driver's seat. For a while longer he studied the image in his rearview mirror.

"I may's well go," Ron finally told himself and turned the ignition key. The cat hastily backed away and disappeared off the road's brushy downhill side.

After stopping by his house to clean the mushrooms, Ron hurried back out to sell them. He wanted to warn his usual buyer, Paulette, about the lion on Mount Arrowsmith so she could pass the word to the other pickers. Besides, he was dying to tell this story.

But Paulette beat him to it. "I hear there was a cougar nosing around your van today," she said.

"How'd you know that?" he asked, confused. He had mentioned the cougar to his sister when she had stopped by as he was cleaning pines, but his sister didn't know Paulette.

The buyer's answer startled Ron as much as anything that had happened on the mountain that day. "A couple other pickers were in. They saw a cougar by your van early this morning."

"Early this morning?"

"Yeah, first thing."

For the first time, Ron felt fear. Buck and Ron hadn't stumbled upon a cougar in the old-growth forest of Mount Arrowsmith, accidentally putting a rude end to a fine day. They had been followed every step of the way. As they had forced their way through second-growth timber so dense that twenty cougars could have hidden in it, as Ron had zigzagged among the old growth with eyes primed to see only mushrooms—for three hours or more—they had been shadowed by a predator. Ron remembered how Buck had stayed close all morning, as though he knew.

Nobody in Port Alberni had a cougar story this good.

19

STALKED BY A MOUNTAIN LION?

Bowhunter Steve Carmichael was scouting for elk in eastern Oregon in the fall of 1999 when he noticed an acrid odor. It reminded him of old kitty litter. Then he saw the cougar, lying in a slight depression ten feet away. As they made eye contact, it snarled and disappeared into the brush.

Steve decided it was time for him to leave, too. He stepped across a small creek and made his way to a barbed-wire fence about half a mile away. There he sat to rest and think about what he'd seen.

Unbelievably, here was a large brown animal standing in the trail he'd just left, staring at him. The second cougar sighting of his life, barely ten minutes after the first. Could it be the same animal? Had he been followed? Fighting a momentary urge to flee, Steve rose and lifted his bow, growling. Then he noticed, close behind the big cat, a spotted kitten. Bears defend their young. Maybe cougars did, too. Steve began to think he might be in real trouble.

Then another adult cougar appeared behind the first two. This was way too much. Weren't cougars supposed to be solitary? Steve took two careful steps back. The nearest, largest cat took two steps forward.

Steve glanced down to nock an arrow. When he lifted his eyes the cat was much closer. Steve stepped back again. As he did, he couldn't help it: He reflexively glanced behind to check for rocks or logs. When he looked up, the cat had glided closer yet.

If someone was about to be hurt, Steve decided, he'd rather it be the cougar. He drew his bow and let fly. The cougar crouched; the arrow whizzed past. Despite the arrow's landing clatter, the animal continued to stare. The man shot again. This arrow grazed the cat's left shoulder. It startled back into the forest, followed by its companions.

Five miles away and two days further into their annual family hunt, Steve's son Greg starred in the sequel. Scouting alone, Greg faced first one, then a second full-sized cougar. He yelled, cursed, and raised his bow over his head. Steve heard his son's shouts through the fading light, "Get out of here. Go away. Leave me alone!"

Greg fired an arrow but missed. Again the cougars left. Steve and Greg decided to end their hunt early.

Some call them stalkings. Others dislike the word. It implies that the animal hunts the human it follows, an unproven assumption. The facts are these: Most serious cougar attacks begin from ambush, not as a culmination of a staring confrontation; and no human who has been stalked but not attacked can know whether attack was imminent. Those who've had this experience, however, say that being followed by a predator has a way of making a person feel like prey.

Consider these four recent stories that define the range of disturbing cougar encounters. What sets them apart from incidental sightings is that the cat seems to be in charge. What makes them different from attacks is that the cougar never makes physical contact, although it may do everything but. While they seldom involve more than one cat—in that, the Carmichaels' twin encounters are bizarre—stalking encounters are not particularly uncommon. Stories like these can be found with a quick search through the archives of any western newspaper. These happen to come from the Spokane, Washington, daily, the *Spokesman-Review*, whose circulation area includes rich deer and cougar habitat.

Shaun Johnson, dropping newspapers for delivery outside Spokane at 3:30 A.M., glanced up to see a cougar emerge from the woods. Although it could have circled, invisible, through forest, the animal instead walked across open ground past Shaun, and continued toward the lakefront homes the papers were destined for. It showed no interest in the man, but no fear either. Shaun nervously hopped into his van, shut the door, and watched the animal glide across his rearview mirror.

A Forest Service worker hiking alone one morning had a more intimidating experience. He was followed by a cougar for half an hour at a distance of perhaps thirty yards. The animal sometimes circled the man and sometimes trailed him, but never approached. It disappeared before other Forest Service workers arrived.

Russell Maas and his fourteen-year-old nephew were scouting game near Moyie Springs, Idaho, when a cougar burst from the brush and sprinted straight at them. It stopped ten yards away, crouched, and growled. The two yelled and waved their arms, but the cougar didn't budge. Finally Russell, remembering an old cougar hunter's tale, barked like a dog. The cougar fled.

Darrell Brazington and his adult stepson were approached by a cougar as they surveyed timber near Priest River, Idaho. The men tried barking, waving their arms, and yelling, but the big cat kept coming. Finally, Darrell told his stepson to take off his shirt. They wrapped it around a stick and set it afire. The cougar wheeled away from the makeshift torch, but shadowed the men at a distance of fifty feet as they hiked to safety.

These encounters made newspaper headlines because the people involved reported them. But most people who capture cougars' attention don't report their encounters for one simple reason: They don't know they had them.

Cougar hunter Bob Sheppard once followed a cat's track into a new rural subdivision near Missoula, Montana. Standing in the cougar's round paw prints, he found he was staring into a lit basement window. He was sure that the animal too had paused to stare inside. Then he followed the tracks across the backyard and out of the subdivision. He figured that the homeowners, who had driven away perhaps forty-five minutes earlier, had probably been watched as they climbed into their vehicle.

Cougar hunters often find, as they retrace their steps homeward, that the day's freshest cougar sign lies atop their own boot prints. Although this happens often enough that cougar hunters joke about it, it's a rare hunter who actually sees the trailing animal.

"How can I be out in the hills as much as I am and never see [cougars]? There's a fascination in the fact that I can't see them, but they're watching me," mused longtime Montana houndsman Ed Roche.

In the sparsely populated central Montana country Ed hunts, cougars are easy to find. He could tree a cat almost every good tracking day if he wanted. He and his hunting friends have many, many photographs and videotapes of wild cougars, but the subjects are all in trees with hounds barking up at them.

"If a cougar follows you really close, you might see it. But if he stays twenty-five yards away, you'll probably never know," said Idaho houndsman Steve Ryan.

Cougars and cougar stories abound in the tiny central Idaho town of Lowell where Steve and his wife, Anne, live. The Ryans run a small café called the Wilderness Inn. On one wall hangs an eight-foot-long cougar hide, its head and densely furred tail still attached. In plain view across the river is the glass phone booth in which, says Anne, a camper once took refuge as a cougar prowled past and into a busy resort's grassy campground.

Anne recounted a local story about two hunters scouting for game on parallel ridgelines. One man fired his weapon in the direction of the other, a friendship-straining offense to say the least. Later, the shooter reduced his irate friend to stunned silence by explaining that he'd fired at a cougar ghosting close behind the man.

Hunting guide, tracker, and houndsman Tom Parker lives in Montana's Swan Valley. He believes cougars have a natural aversion to humans that makes us unattractive as prey, but says, "It's not at all uncommon for cats to . . . investigate humans."

Tom chooses his words carefully. "Stalk" or even "follow" sound too alarmist. Tom wants to give cougars the benefit of the doubt—particularly, he points out, since most cougars have passed up many opportunities to attack people.

"If I were a lion and I looked at these helpless, slow-moving, unobservant beings, I don't think I'd resist the temptation," says Tom. Yet cougars do exactly that all the time.

Tom has an encounter story, too. One spring day, he was scouting for bear on a steep, west-facing slope. Logged off long ago, the slope was shrubby and dotted with ten-foot-tall ponderosa pines, which made visibility poor. Movement drew his eye to a half dozen mule deer bunched together. They were staring intently at a point below and to Tom's right. Tom pays attention to animal eyes: They show him things. Sure enough, concealed beneath a pine tree seventy yards from Tom, watched nervously by the deer, was a mountain lion. At almost the same moment Tom saw the lion, it caught sight of him through the brush and began gliding in his direction.

Tom thought he knew what was happening. With their several pairs of eyes all focused on the cat, the deer were difficult prey. But Tom was alone and too obscured by foliage to be identified as a human. The hunter stepped left, trying to make himself visible through a break in the brush. The cougar responded by turning into a shallow draw.

A less savvy woodsman might have thought the lion gone, but Tom saw that the draw would bring the animal, invisible, nearly to his feet. It wasn't leaving; it was hunting. Tom turned to face the spot where, if he had guessed right, the cougar would appear. Minutes later, a round head emerged from the brush. The eyes were fixed on Tom.

"I'm confident that cat didn't know I was human," says Tom. "It had only seen little movements through the brush. I was apprehensive, but I thought that once it realized what I was, I could deter it."

The hunter stepped up onto a log. "Hey, you. Get out of here," he yelled. The cat instantly deflated, spun toward its tail, and disappeared.

It seems Tom was right: This cougar did not want to hunt a human. But is that true of all cats which approach people but don't make contact? If so, why approach them at all? What's in it for the cougar?

In early spring of 1999, Tom and his wife Mel took the authors of an earlier version of this book looking for cats. A day-old dusting over a firm snow base made for good tracking, and the party soon crossed fresh sign. But the animal's wide, round footprints were not the only marks on the isolated logging road: The cat's tracks paralleled—and sometimes lay atop—the twin rails left by a lone-cross country skier.

With a practiced gesture, Tom produced a tape measure. A few moments later he announced the tracks had probably been left by an adult female. Adult males are a third larger than females, with proportionately larger paws and a longer stride.

To find out how the cougar came to place her feet in the skier's trail, our group back-trailed her. Ten minutes' snowshoeing led into dense forest and, finally, to a cougar daybed, an irregular oval depression in the snow beneath a fir. It was situated on a hillside so heavily used by deer that the cold air was sharp with their scent.

Tom read for us the story written in the snow. The cat had exploded from her bed with huge bounds of twelve feet or more. Then she slowed to a ground-eating trot aimed straight at the logging road, invisible but only a quarter mile away. Tom speculated aloud that the cougar had heard the skier's shush-shushing and hurried to investigate.

The two trails first met near where we had initially crossed them. The cat's track followed the skier's from that point for two hundred yards. Then the cougar's veered left, back into heavy forest. The skier's trail continued out of sight around a bend in the road.

She got bored, we speculated aloud, and wandered off on other cougar business. Tom didn't comment. He simply turned to follow the round paw prints into the trees. It quickly became clear that her track made a beeline through the brush, effectively shortcutting the switchback. After the curve, the cat's tracks rejoined the skier's.

We followed her next shortcut as well. It bypassed a massive squiggling meander in the old logging road, saving her perhaps a mile. On a high bank before she rejoined the road, Tom found the cougar's only stopping place. She had stood, perhaps for quite a while, shifting her feet now and then but not sitting or crouching. It was hard not to imagine that she waited for the skier, now behind her because of her shortcut.

If so, she gave up and stepped onto the road too early, because for a short distance the cat's tracks were *beneath* the skier's.

A dozen yards later, the animal had leapt aside into dense brush and then returned to the road. Now the cat's tracks were again atop those of the skier, as though she had hidden to let the skier pass so she could again follow.

A half-mile after that, the cougar left the road again, this time for good. She headed into a thicket where layers of tracks said she often spent time. Deer trails laced the area as well. The ski tracks continued down the road, presumably to their owner's car.

Tom points out that this cat used a good part of her day to follow this lone human, ultimately without bothering him. More interesting yet, she knew the skier would stay on the road, and that if she shortcutted the road she would leapfrog the skier. How? She had to have watched people often enough to be able to predict their actions.

Some encounters, especially in remote areas, seem more like attempts to puzzle out a creature never before observed. In August of 1996 a young river guide named Dave O'Keefe hitchhiked up central Idaho's Lochsa River to a trailhead he knew well from regular solitary backpacking trips. Across the Lochsa sprawled the Selway-Bitterroot Wilderness, one of few places in the country still wild enough to support grizzlies. Dave headed away from designated wilderness and toward country just as wild: Clearwater country, one of the most arduous legs of the original Lewis and Clark Trail.

Five miles in, he reached the flat area where he planned to camp. An old miner's cabin shared the brushy clearing. Dave figured that was because the builder had had no choice: In this rugged country, there were no other flat spots for miles.

Always careful about attracting wildlife, Dave hung his food from the log bridge that crossed Fish Creek. Then he lay out his bedding. Not much for tents, Dave liked trees and sky for bedroom walls and ceiling.

At 3:00 A.M., the young man woke with a vague sense of urgency. He took stock: He lay on his back, legs straight, arms tucked into his mummy bag against the damp mountain chill. No sound disturbed the stillness. He let his eyes open and immediately felt his heart accelerate. Above and behind him, a large shape blocked stars. A dog, he thought. A wolf? Whatever it was, it was too damn close.

He was afraid to free his hands—the zipper would buzz—so he rolled rapidly to his knees, facing what now stood motionless only a few feet away: a full-grown, honest-to-God cougar.

The cat backed away two steps. Dave, heart thudding, began talking quietly. "Take it easy, buddy. Take it easy."

Enough moonlight pooled in the clearing that Dave could begin to make out the animal's tensed muscles and narrowed eyes. It didn't look any happier than he was. If it attacked, Dave told himself, he'd duke it in the nose.

"I grew up surfing in shark-infested waters and that's what I'd always heard—give 'em one good punch in the nose and they'll go away."

The fact that his hands were still trapped in the sleeping bag didn't register with the five-feet-five, 130-pound man until much later. The fact that the cat looked huge did. Twenty seconds passed. Then its muscles visibly relaxed. It turned and paced slowly toward the black wall of forest.

Dave knew the encounter was over. The cat's body language was telling him so. Fear evaporated, and he began trying to record what suddenly seemed a painfully lovely thing, the cat lit by moonlight, gliding away, its feet placed with light precision. He wished it would look back so he could memorize its face as well. It didn't.

Hear enough of these stories and you find yourself begging for answers. Such encounters are a recurring and probably important part of the cougar/human dynamic. Yet any animal that, over time, expends more energy than it consumes will die. And plenty of cougars do starve, bankrupted by this harsh accounting system. What then does a cougar mean to accomplish by following humans? Why waste the energy? Are stalkings attacks that almost happened? Are attacks stalking incidents during which the oblivious human did something wrong?

The search for reasonable answers is blocked by the comforting (but probably false) belief that cougars have an innate or learned fear of humans. If cougars are "supposed" to fear humans, any cougar which follows a human is by definition abnormal and abnormality becomes the simple answer.

Longtime cougar hunters like Steve Ryan and Doug Caltrider say cats have a natural fear of hounds but not of hunters. Doug once stayed to watch a treed tom after the dogs were led away.

"It was just like you flipped a switch back on," he said. "He'd been cowering on a branch and then he stood up, pricked his ears and looked down as if to say, 'Buddy, I ain't scared of you. I'm not up here 'cause of you.'"

Here's one possible explanation for cougar stalkings. Predators like African lions and wolves sometimes show themselves to their prey before attacking. Some think the predator is deliberately seeking a fear reaction. An animal that shows no fear may be telegraphing the fact that it is healthy and alert, a difficult adversary. The fearful animal may betray, by its fear, the fact that it is less able to flee or fight effectively. Naturalist Barry Lopez has even wondered, in *Of Wolves and Men*, if predator and prey don't collaborate in the moments before attack. An ill or old caribou might be grateful for a fast finish instead of slow starvation, and the wolf grateful for being pointed to an easy, safe kill.

If cougars are like these predators, stalking and charging could be the cougar's attempt to ask the all-important question: Are you my meat? Unable to see ourselves inhabiting the painful end of the food chain, perhaps we send back unreadable answers. The animal follows, encouraged neither to attack nor to give up.

Or it could be that cougars are confused by similarities and differences between humans and deer. As has been said elsewhere in this book, cougars seem hard-wired to prefer deer: Humans, like deer, can be found along trails or in clearings. Both species are often found near water. Both travel in groups. Individuals are approximately the same size.

But they are not the same shape and this, some believe, is why cougar attacks are so rare. Perhaps cautious cougars hesitate to attack something that lacks the four legs and long, ungulate neck of a deer. The cougar might follow humans out of predatory interest but keep a safe distance out of caution.

Perhaps stalking has nothing to do with hunting. Wolves and dogs use stiff-legged displays to assert and hold social position in a pack. Bears posture to keep the best fishing spot in a river or to warn other bears away from cubs. Bear attacks upon humans are often preceded by signals such as loud jaw popping or false charges. Perhaps the humans attacked after such warnings didn't respond in a way that satisfied the bear. If, for instance, the correct response from another bear would have been a noisy twenty-five-mile-per-hour retreat, the human's fumbling backward walk may appear insultingly casual.

When cougars communicate among themselves about who has to leave an area, perhaps stalking and charging are part of the vocabulary. Or perhaps stalking is a cougar's response when a human doesn't acknowledge an attempt at communication—a scent marker perhaps—that the human couldn't "read." A cougar crouched on a road bank, staring intently at a person, may be screaming in cougarese, "Can't you hear me? Get the hell off my porch, you social incompetent. You're scaring away my deer."

Author Richard Conniff offers a friendlier explanation for stalkings, courtesy of biologist Sarah Durant of the Serengeti Cheetah Research Project. Watching two cheetahs which stopped to observe antelope and wildebeest but did not give chase, their bellies rounded with a recent meal, Sarah said, "I often think they watch prey the way we watch television, because it's comforting and mindless."

We can find support for Sarah's theory much closer to home: Domestic cats show endless interest in things that move. Perhaps a moving human interests a cougar in the same way a drifting leaf or a goldfish in a bowl entrances a house cat.

But is this curiosity indeed idle or does it indicate a more purposeful interest? Paul Leyhausen and others have experimented with house cats and captive wild species and found that a cat will chase, catch, and kill mice long after it is full. It may stop killing after a while but it will continue chasing and catching. Then it may stop catching but continue to chase.

The explanation lies in what successful hunters do with their time, says Leyhausen. Most predators chase more animals than they catch, and catch more than they manage to kill. If they are females with young, they kill more than they eat. The same is true if other predators steal their kills. If it were only the eating that gave a predator pleasure, most of its life would be unsatisfying. It may be that successful predators are rewarded at every step in the hunt, from stalk to kill to belly full of meat, with a sensation we might recognize as joy.

Perhaps the cougar behavior known as "surplus killing" is explainable in this light. When a cougar kills a dozen or more milling sheep, feeding on perhaps one or none at all, it may be that the herd's behavior or availability triggers a compulsion which the cougar cannot resist. He could kill one sheep and spend his night feeding upon it, seemingly a much more sensible use of his time, but instead he spends it killing and killing and killing.

Are people who are stalked in danger? Almost certainly yes, and certainly more than if no cougar silently watched. No matter why the cougar follows, a predator can't afford to go long without killing. At some point as it silently trails a hiker down a brushy path, surely it considers its options.

And almost always, after long minutes or even hours of shadowing a human whose senses are too weak to tell him he's not alone, this magnificently efficient, powerful carnivore turns his back and strolls away.

20

HARD LESSONS

In 1998 Wes Collins lived in forested foothills outside Issaquah, a bedroom community near Seattle. Washington has had its share of well-publicized cougar attacks, most involving children. But Wes didn't worry much about his four kids. He had a dog. Then in May of 1998, a 145-pound cougar attacked and killed his part-Labrador retriever within yards of the house. It dragged the dog's body fifty yards into cover. The next morning when state Fish and Game agents arrived, the cougar was still there. Agents tried to tree it with their hounds but it attacked those dogs as well, according to the *Seattle Times*.

People in cougar country hold other understandable misconceptions about cougars as well. For instance, it's an understandable error to think a family dog ensures against cougar attack. Cougars, after all, are hunted with hounds. Less well known is the fact that they kill and eat dogs of all sizes.

Others think that if their pets don't protect them, they can at least protect their pets with a fence or a leash or perhaps just by keeping an eye on them. But California biologist and author Steven Torres says pet attacks are increasingly common. Pets are taken from yards, decks, and porches. Some, on morning strolls with their owners, are yanked right out of their collars. One cougar walked into a mountain resort's store through the open back door to snatch a puppy that was playing at a woman's feet.

Twenty-year-old Joshua Rhoden was running three dogs, including a half-grown rottweiler-chow, behind his truck near Olympic National Park, Washington, when he saw a huge, tawny animal bounding behind the dogs. The cougar grabbed the stocky pup and sprang into a roadside ditch. Joshua stopped his truck and ran back to throw rocks and scream at the cougar. It did not release the dog. Joshua finally got scared and gave up, according to the *Peninsula Daily News*.

Especially after an attack or rash of sightings, news programs broadcast safety advice, warning signs appear at trailheads, and park rangers dispense cougar safety pamphlets. But sound bites, signs, and leaflets can be misleading or flat-out incorrect. By necessity they are short and simple, and safety among large predators is not simple.

In fact, the wealth of cougar safety information creates, simply by existing, the biggest misconception of all. It makes cougar attack appear a significant risk. Otherwise, why waste all that ink, agency expense, and airtime?

The point of cougar safety advice, however, is not that attack risk is significant but that people feel more secure when they have some control over their level of risk. In that spirit, the rest of this chapter is devoted to rendering the advice in cougar safety brochures more useful, and pointing out where it is probably not.

Noise and human bustle make people feel secure, partly because intuition says it should, and partly because safety brochures advise hikers and runners to travel with others. But while groups are a good idea, they don't prevent all attacks, especially on kids. Sixteen of nineteen 1990s child victims were in groups when attacked. Some were in large, noisy clusters, hiking at the end of a line of children and camp counselors, like Dante Swallow, or running through a church camp with other children, like the little girl attacked by a half-grown kitten in Hope, British Columbia.

That's why another frequent cougar country warning—to keep children close—can be misleading. There is a good reason to keep kids close and travel in groups, but it's not that companions *prevent* attack. Researcher Lee Fitzhugh found that children in groups were just slightly less at risk of attack than children alone. The reason to keep children close is that companions can *end* attacks.

Of the two documented 1990s cases in which kids died, Mark Miedema was hiking perhaps four minutes ahead of his parents when attacked. And Jeremy Williams was sitting with three other students at the edge of a schoolyard in Kyuquot, British Columbia. When the children's screams summoned adult help, the school custodian shot the cat off the boy. But fatal damage had already been done.

Since 2000 no child victim has been alone when attacked. And no child victim has died.

Lee Fitzhugh, relying on work done by Kenny Logan and Linda Sweanor on radio-collared cats, believes that cougars are in fact less likely to approach humans in a group but that, once a cougar is in close proximity, the fact that humans are grouped will not necessarily deter an attack if the right kind of "trigger," say a running child, is present.

One amazing fact that some cougar safety brochures leave out altogether, perhaps to prevent lawsuits, is that rescuers are almost never badly hurt. They usually aren't even scratched. When bears attack, would-be rescuers often become victims too, as though the provoked bear simply needs to fight and any target will do. It would be an easy mistake to make, thinking that cougars would follow the same pattern, and several would-be rescuers have hung back, fearful.

But some successful rescuers have only needed to shout. John Musselman was barefoot and empty-handed when he charged his son's attacker. It evaporated before him like a ghost. More often rescuers must use force, but their weapons don't have to be fancy. Nine-year-old Darron Arroyo's dad smashed a rock onto the head of a cougar that was dragging his son away. The cougar dropped the boy and fled. In Nevada, Mary Saethre was rescued by one companion while another stood by, perhaps frozen by the understandable belief that a real weapon was needed. He could find only a rock. Meanwhile, Paul Greger drove Mary's seventy-pound attacker off by hitting it repeatedly with his camera. None of these rescuers reported receiving even a scratch.

If it sounds odd that such a formidable predator could be deterred by a camera or that hand-to-hand combat with a cougar could have a happy ending, consider this: Even a deer sometimes can stand off its nemesis, as raft guide Shane Duncan witnessed one summer day in 1997.

Shane was on a commercial wilderness trip down Idaho and Oregon's Snake River. The rafts were stopped at a spot called Deep Creek when guests noticed a doe and two fawns climbing precariously up a ravine on the river's far side. As the group watched, one of the fawns suddenly tumbled downhill in a cloud of dust.

It took Shane a moment to realize that another animal had caused the fall. In that moment, the doe attacked. She reared onto her hind legs, flailing with heart-shaped hooves, forcing whatever it was away from her fawn and up into a brambly hackberry tree. Then she backed away to stand guard before the crumpled fawn.

The rafters were horrified and enthralled. Who would have thought a deer could fight off, well, a whatever-it-was? Something small, Shane figured, small enough to be afraid of a deer. Bobcat, maybe?

For fifteen minutes, the doe faced the tree. The little bobcat didn't budge. If the doe hoped the fragile tangle of legs at her back would rise and rejoin its sibling, she waited in vain. It never stirred. Finally she turned, gathered her remaining fawn, and exited the ravine. The animal in the tree immediately bounded down, and Shane saw it clearly for the first time. It was much larger than he'd expected. It had a brown stripe down its back and a long, thick brown tail. The cougar lifted the limp fawn by its neck and carried it behind a rock.

This scene raises a possible explanation for the cougar's characteristic readiness to be driven from prey. With patience and no further risk on the cougar's part, the wounded often become meat.

Another aspect of cougar conflict seldom mentioned in safety brochures is the animal's determined focus. Cats chased away from injured children return again and again. They try to sneak between a rescuer's legs, as did the cougar that attacked Dante Swallow. When Lila Lifely made the mistake of leaving the child she had rescued to retrieve first-aid gear, the cougar immediately returned to the girl. Possibly it's this unswerving focus that keeps rescuers safe: The cougar sees them as obstacles, nothing more.

One piece of questionable advice offered by most cougar safety brochures is this: "When confronted by an aggressive cougar, make yourself appear larger. Raise your pack or coat over your head." I have so far not met the person who has successfully frightened off a cougar by raising his arms or opening his coat. Cougars are sight hunters with amazing depth perception. It's true that when people in standoffs with cougars fall down, bend over, or turn their backs, the action can trigger attack. But it's unlikely that the trigger is an apparent change in the person's size. More likely it's the appearance of vulnerability.

Suzanne Groves was collecting stream samples near Cortez, Colorado, when she noticed she was being eyed by a cougar. She began wading the shallow Mancos River toward her vehicle. The cat matched her, step for step. The woman splashed water and yelled. The cat merely continued to pace her. When Suzanne stumbled on the slick rocks, she lost sight of the cat. The next instant, she felt the animal bite into the back of her head, forcing her face underwater.

Luckily for her, the cougar was old, nearly toothless and, at sixty-three pounds, well underweight. The woman wrestled herself free. When she ran for the bank, she was tackled again. Again she fought free. She finally stabbed the animal in the eye with a pair of fisherman's forceps. The cougar gave up the attack and Suzanne scrambled away and escaped to her vehicle.

Hikers and bikers are often told that noise can frighten off aggressive cougars, but not necessarily what kind of noise. There is a difference. Lee Fitzhugh and colleagues, after compiling and studying cougar attack records, wrote in 2003 that yelling seems far more effective at deterring attack than gunshots. In 74 percent of cases in which people screamed and yelled, the cougar either left the area or backed off. Only 17 percent of cougars left an area after a single shot was fired. Multiple shots were more effective, but still not as effective as yelling.

The short, simple descriptions of cougar behavior listed in brochures make it easy to overgeneralize. Cougars tend to be shy, yes. They would rather not move about during the day. They are generally solitary. But the pair of cougars you meet on the trail at one in the afternoon has not read the brochure. These animals are as unique as you or me. Some cougars retreat when confronted. Others crouch and growl. Some back off at loud shouting. Others become aggressive. Some cougar mothers will attempt to defend their kittens if you approach the birth den.

Most will not. Most cougars will melt away once seen. Others will sit and stare. A very, very few will attack.

Others, faced with every temptation, will not. On May 23, 2006, a six-year-old Vancouver Island boy named Bryce Forbes saw a cougar crouched in his yard. Frightened for his two-year-old brother, he ran forty or fifty feet straight past the animal. He then ran past the cat again, hauling the smaller boy. The two made it safely into their house. It's believed that running—particularly when a child is doing the running—triggers a predatory response. But this cougar did not move. Bryce received a bravery award from British Columbia's environment minister, but it was the cougar's restraint as much as the boy's courage that created a happy ending that day.

Cougar brochures point out that mountain lions are crepuscular, meaning they are most active around dawn and dusk. California's Department of Fish and Game's brochure, "Living with California Mountain Lions," says parents should "make sure children are inside between dusk and dawn." This tip makes it easy to assume that cougar-country residents are safe during the day. But perhaps simply because of sheer numbers—many, many times more humans are about in daylight than at night—nearly all cougar attacks have occurred during daylight hours. It's possible that one significant reason cougar attacks are rare is that we are creatures of the day and they of the night.

Safety brochures always make the point that cougar attacks are very rare. Bear attacks are more common. Dog attacks are more common. Lightning strike is more common. Fatal bee sting is more common. However it's said, the point in these brochures is always that, whatever your level of concern, it's probably out of proportion to the actual risk. Fitzhugh and his coauthors point out that while the risk of cougar conflict, including attack, is small, "Statistics that compare the frequency of puma attacks with that of some other phenomenon, such as lightning strikes, are misleading." The urban resident walking through a subway terminal is at far less risk of attack than the statistics would say. The hiker who, unknowing, passes a hungry mother cougar which has hunted unsuccessfully for three days is surely at more.

Perhaps the biggest misconception in cougar country, fed by common sense and media handling, is that cougars that attack people are abnormal in some way. It's true that a percentage of attacks involve young or malnourished cougars. But most of those attacks seem to follow a distinct "hit and run" pattern. One example is Annette Hayes, who was sitting on her deck near Durango, Colorado, one evening in 2005. Her husband sat at her side and the family dog lay at her feet. Suddenly she felt weight on her shoulders and then a stabbing pain. She screamed and ran for the door. The dislodged cougar dove off the deck and disappeared.

Trackers could not locate the animal, but if he was a typical hit and run cougar, he was subadult and visibly malnourished. The typical hit and run victim, like Annette, suffers a few scratches and puncture wounds but is not seriously injured.

Serious cougar attacks most commonly involve animals who, when necropsied, appear to have been normal, healthy, and adult. Or at least that pattern has held for the last two decades. As has been said earlier in this book, species change as their environment changes. The cougar of tomorrow will be different from the cougar of today. A cougar in Arizona is different from a cougar on Vancouver Island. And every cougar, like every human, is shaped by personal experience.

Washington Department of Fish and Wildlife's Terry Ray-Smith has been an enforcement officer for twenty-one years. She says even the cougar's well-known reticence is changing, at least in northeast Washington where she works. Ranchers and hunters, hikers and mountain bikers, all tell her they see cougars more often. Not only that, sightings more often involve a cougar which is actively interested in a person—for instance, watching him intently from the treeline fifty yards away. "In 2000 nobody would have seen that cougar," she says.

Terry believes we are what changed the equation. In northeastern Washington, you'd be hard-pressed to find a wooded drainage without a house in it. Deer graze on lawns and cougars hunt the deer. Roadless areas are shrinking, and snowmobile and ATV traffic have increased dramatically, making even unroaded areas accessible to humans. If cougars in her region wanted to avoid proximity with humans, they could not.

This does not mean that habituation to humans has caused the increase in attacks of the last two decades. It may be much more simple, as longtime cougar researcher Linda Sweanor points out. What if, she says, some tiny percentage of the cougar population has always been more experimental, bolder. Under the right circumstances, those few animals might be bold enough to consider two-legged prey, despite our odd appearance and smell. Once upon a time that animal might never have gotten a compelling opportunity. But in the twenty-first century, sooner or later the opportunity presents itself.

And the awkward fact is that it doesn't matter if he takes advantage of it or not. His species is capable. Which means that if he is seen (and habituation definitely seems to diminish a cougar's unwillingness to be seen) he becomes a management problem.

Believing cougars would never attack humans made people feel comfortable as cougars recovered in the 1970s and 1980s. Over the last fifteen years or more, from Arizona to British Columbia, the rare event of cougar attack has been publicized so thoroughly that some now believe the risk much higher than it is. This is a disservice to the issue, but there has been a payoff as well. We have begun to accept the honest truth: Co-existence with a large predator is no comfortable thing. It's an honesty from which lasting solutions might grow.

AFTERWORD

People need wild places. Whether or not we think we do, we do. We need to be... surrounded by a singing, mating, howling commotion of other species, all of which love their lives as much as we do ours, and none of which could possibly care less about us in our place.

—Barbara Kingsolver
Small Wonder, Essays

When Erik Wenum first came to Kalispell, Montana, as a bear and lion biologist in 1994, he relocated problem bears just like other game officers across the country. Relocation is a notoriously poor bear management tool. But it sells well to the public, which is why it is still done.

Erik learned that if he released bears more than fifteen miles from where they had been captured, his failure rate exceeded 70 percent. The bear would either return or get into the same trouble in a different place. Erik wanted to try something new. His idea made his bosses nervous, but they too were tired of spending man-hours on empty gestures.

What the biologist began to do seems counterintuitive: He still captured and released problem bears, but he no longer transported them out of the area. Instead, he released them as close to their capture site as possible.

First he explained to the landowner who had phoned in the complaint that it was his garbage cans, bird feeder, or unpicked fruit trees that had attracted the bear in the first place. Erik could not solve the problem, but the landowner could. If he installed bear-proof garbage cans or emptied his bird feeder or picked his fruit, the landowner would become part of Erik's new coexistence school for bears. If he chose not to, the bear would flunk and the landowner's problem would continue.

Then Erik released the groggy animal from the culvert trap.

An animal recovering from tranquilizers is unhappy to begin with. But Erik made sure the bear's day went downhill from there. The first thing it encountered in its former private restaurant was Erik, shooting at it point-blank with star rounds. These nonlethal impact rounds hit hard enough to raise bruises, but not to cause any lasting damage, even at five feet.

The groggy, bawling bear would run. As soon as it gained a little distance, Erik could pummel it with beanbags shot from a shotgun. As the bear fled beanbag range, Erik might switch weapons one last time to continue the barrage with rubber bullets.

The important thing was this: Long after Erik no longer heard its crashing flight, the bear was still on familiar turf. It knew how to find food here without entering human space. And it now had a memorable reason to prefer the huckleberry patch to the trash can.

Ten years into Erik's bear program, its success rate is 98 percent. Even bears which attended Erik's school in 1996, its first year, are still choosing berries over garbage. Agencies in other states have adopted his program with similar success. Others are studying it.

Next Erik began to ponder the region's lion problem. Could the same strategy work on a pure carnivore? Clearly landowners would play a more critical role. It wasn't as simple as putting away the feeders. Landowners had to agree to stop feeding the wild turkeys and deer, but they would also have to bring in their pets at night or build them a secure kennel. They might need to quit hobby farming or invest in the heavy-duty fences and barns required to protect their sheep, chickens, or llamas.

Erik's cougar school is taught by hounds that tree the cat repeatedly, but the principle is the same as with his on-site bear releases.

"It's cost-benefit analysis," says Erik. But it's more than that: It's adaptation. Mutual adaptation, which is how natural systems evolve.

Only a handful of cougars have so far attended his school, so Erik doesn't know if it works as well as his bear program. But in 1998 and 1999, he was killing four to five problem lions a month. In the last three years, he has killed none. Some of the change is due to his own perspective shift, his unwillingness to kill cougars for what he now sees as human-created problems; some grows from local residents' greater willingness to adapt; and some of it is probably Erik's cougars passing their final exams.

When I first started following this issue in 1998, my writing partner and I identified two kinds of willful blindness about large predators. The first my partner called "Bambification," referring to the tendency to celebrate large predator recovery while ignoring associated costs or dismissing them as insignificant. People with this attitude tended to think it politically incorrect to ask, for instance, if there might be places where large predators simply should not be tolerated.

The flipside attitude I named "the painted cattle guard," after the stripes painted on country roads that fool cattle into seeing an impassible obstacle. Proponents seemed to see a barrier between the "natural" and the human world. They were often outraged when bears, cougars, and coyotes were spotted in humanscapes, as though the animals had willfully committed trespass.

Today it strikes me that, more than blindness, both attitudes were refusals to adapt.

I believe the cougar, more than most species, demands our adaptation. With their successful recovery, their march east and their explorations of our cities, the big cats are challenging us to make a place for them, sharp claws and all. If we won't, or can't, they will continue to try to carve out a place for themselves.

Leaving aside for a moment the question of *why* we should adapt to cougars, let's ask what this adaptation might look like.

The answers I've read that sound plausible share three points. One is the belief that for cougars to survive we must actively decide as a society that we wish their survival, and support that choice in the ways we use and develop the nation's fast-shrinking reservoirs of open land.

Second, adaptation will involve not just expense to society, but also personal inconvenience and acceptance of a small but deeply disturbing risk. Game agencies will be tasked with limiting that risk even while knowing that they can never eliminate it. That cost accrues to each individual resident of cougar country.

Third, answers will not grow out of popular wisdom or wishful thinking but solid research, much of which remains to be done. And it can't be done just once. Cougar behavior changes. Very few predicted the explosion of cougar attacks in the 1990s. Those who did were called alarmist. Fewer would have predicted, thirty years ago, that cougars would utilize cities and suburbs as they do. The cougars which do so can't be managed based on studies done decades ago on remote public lands.

As for why we might choose to share our world with cougars, I don't think biologists can help much. Scientists try hard to come up with objective, logical arguments as to why problematic species like cougars should survive. I've not heard one yet that stands up against a developer's money or a parent's fear for his child.

Nevertheless, if we refuse this resilient predator his comeback, we will be diminished.

We've proven again and again that we're not smart enough to monkey with natural systems. From toads to trout, our tinkering has almost always produced unintended and often tragic repercussions. Extinction is irreversible, and the world becomes smaller with each species we eliminate from it.

Less concretely, a world in which man is the only predator just feels wrong. Without large predators, wouldn't the woods seem less deep and shadowed, more like a theme park? We evolved huddled around a sheltering fire. What would we become without the primal fear that drove us to that ring of light?

As a society we must decide whether to shoulder the costs of coexistence, and take clear-eyed responsibility for that choice. But each individual most choose as well: a safe world where you need not modify your behavior or a more challenging world in which you must sometimes move with humility, a world large enough for predators like cougars.

I don't know which world we will choose but I'm sure of this: Along the way we will test the limits of the cougar's adaptability. And he will test ours.

SOURCES AND ACKNOWLEDGMENTS

A book like this requires picking the brains of hundreds of people. Those below were particularly generous with their time, expertise, and, in some cases, their painful memories. To the extent that this book captured an accurate picture of coexistence with cougars, credit goes to them; any mistakes are mine.

Key witnesses and sources helped bring the stories in this book to life. They include Dave O'Keefe; Jim Mepham; Shane Duncan; Mike and Marie Smith; Gold River residents Suzanne Trevis, Ingrid Dahl, Carol Volk, Denise Watt, Barb Jackson, Cynthia Montgomery, Dale Frame, Bonnie and Chelsea Bellwood, Doug Kennedy, Peter Skilton, Dan McInnes; Jerry West, editor of the *Gold River Record;* Anne Fiddick, mayor of Gold River; Port Alberni residents Bill Brown, Ron and Heather Receveur, and Norm Nelson; *Alberni Valley Times* Editor Karen Beck; Karen Hanna; Garnet Parker; Jim and Karen Manion; Russ Bravard and Ernie Flores; Lucy Oberlin; Lona Kottle; Chuck and Cindy Traisi of Fund for Animals; Aaron Hall; Lila Lifely; Steve Carmichael; Christina Kafka; Richard Staskus; Tim Loewen and David Woodward of Victoria, British Columbia's, Empress Hotel; Craig Grebicki.

Cougar hunters and trackers shared their intimate knowledge of cougars. They include Montanans Tom and Mel Parker, Tiger Hulett, Doug Caltrider, Ed Roche, Howard Copenhaver, Bob Sheppard, Bud

Martin, and Bob Wiesner; Steve and Ann Ryan of Idaho; Dan Lay of British Columbia; Dave Fjelline of California; Lyle Wilmarth of Colorado; and Frank Smith of New Mexico.

Game managers, researchers, and wildlife enforcement officers shared their perspective and experience. They include retired California Fish and Game Lt. Bob Turner; retired Washington Department of Fish and Wildlife Sgt. Ray Kahler; Laura Itogawa, superintendent, Cuyamaca Rancho State Park; Montana biologist Eric Wenum; researchers Paul Beier, Dave Choate, Jim Halfpenny, E. Lee Fitzhugh, David Shackleton, Mike Puzzo, Maurice Hornocker, Toni Ruth, Kenny Logan, and Linda Sweanor; cougar incident collector Linda Lewis; John Phelps of Arizona Department of Fish and Game; Steven Torres of California Department of Fish and Game; Todd Malmsbury and Anna Bazquez of the Colorado Division of Wildlife; Doug Caldwell of Rocky Mountain National Park; Jon Rachael and Mark Drew of Idaho Department of Fish and Game and Idaho Wildlife Health Laboratory, respectively; Rich DeSimone of Montana's Department of Fish, Wildlife and Parks; San Juan Stiver of Nevada Department of Game and Fish; Chuck Hayes of New Mexico Department of Game and Fish; Don Whittaker of Oregon Department of Fish and Wildlife; Paul B. Robertson and Raymond Skiles of Texas Parks and Wildlife and Big Bend National Park, respectively; Bill Bates and Steve Cranney of Utah Division of Wildlife Resources; Washington Department of Fish and Wildlife's Steve Pozzanghera, Sean Carrell, Margaret Ainscough, Madonna Luer, Terry Ray-Smith and Jim Rieck; Dave Moody of Wyoming Game and Fish Department; Bruce Treichel and Drew Mahaffey of Alberta Ministry of Environment; Matt Austin, Lance Sundquist, Kim Brunt, and Doug Janz of British Columbia Ministry of Environment; British Columbia conservation officers Gerry Brunham, Pat Brown Clayton, and Bob Smirl; British Columbia RCMP officer Bill Bellwood; Walter Howard; California game wardens and capture experts Bob Pirtle, Sean Pirtle, and Bob Teagle; California park rangers Bob Hillis, Stan Banksen, and Donna Krucki; California park administrators Mark Jorgensen, Tim Miller, and Jim Burke; Lynn Sadler of the Mountain Lion Foundation in California; USDA Wildlife Services Officer Jeff Brent. Eastern cougar background came from Virginia

Department of Game and Inland Fisheries biologists Rick Reynolds and Matt Knox; Cougar Quest Director Barbara Chapin; writer Chris Bolgiano; Shenandoah National Park biologist Jim Atkinson; West Virginia Environmental Resource Specialist Jack Wallace; the Eastern Cougar Foundation's Todd Lester.

Attack victims and their families deserve special note. They agreed to delve into difficult memories, usually out of a desire to teach people about living with cougars. I hope this book honors their trust. Thanks go to Bill White and his family; the Parolin family; the Schoener family; Kyle Musselman and his family; the Small family; the Mellon family; the survivors of Iris Kenna; Marv Waanders, uncle to Mark Miedema; Jason Underdahl and his family; Joel Anderson and his family; Dante Swallow and his family; Johnny Wilson and his family. This book wouldn't exist without Dean Miller, coauthor of the first version, who gave me permission to do as I wished with both the book and our shared research.

A special thank you goes to readers whose sharp ear and conscientious attention shows on every page of this book. They are Falcon editors Leah Gilman and Allen Jones; and gracious volunteers Angie Feinstein, Mark Ives, and, as always, Barry Rabin. Barry, thanks for all the BLTs. There is no amount of tired a home-grown tomato sandwich can't cure.

BIBLIOGRAPHY

Books and documents that informed my thinking include but are not limited to the following:

Aune, Keith. "Lion Report 98." CD-Rom presentation.

Baron, David. *The Beast in the Garden: A Modern Parable of Man and Nature.* New York and London: W.W. Norton & Company, 2004.

Barrett, Reginald H., and Paul Beier. "The Cougar in the Santa Ana Mountain Range, California." Final Report of the Orange County Cooperative Mountain Lion Study, 1993.

Beier, Paul. "A Checklist for Evaluating Impacts to Wildlife Movement Corridors." Wildlife Society Bulletin, 1992.

————. "Cougar Attacks on Humans: An Update and Some Further Reflections." Proceedings of the 15th Vertebrate Pest Conference, University of California, Davis, 1992.

————. "Cougar Attacks on Humans in the United States and Canada." Wildlife Society Bulletin, 1991.

————. "Determining Minimum Habitat Areas and Habitat Corridors for Cougars." *Conservation Biology,* 1993.

————. "Dispersal of Juvenile Cougars in Fragmented Habitat." *Journal of Wildlife Management,* 1995.

————, with Dave Choate and Reginald Barrett. "Movement Patterns of Mountain Lions during Different Behaviors." *Journal of Mammalogy,* 1995.

Bolgiano, Chris. *Mountain Lion: An Unnatural History of Pumas and People*. Mechanicsburg, Pa: Stackpole Books, 1995.

————. with Jerry Roberts. *The Eastern Cougar*. Mechanicsburg, Pa.: Stackpole Books, 2005.

Busch, Robert. *The Cougar Almanac: A Complete Natural History of the Mountain Lion*. New York: Lyons and Burford, 1996.

Cougar Management Guidelines. Cougar Management Guidelines Working Group. Bainbridge Island, Wash.: Wildfutures, 2005.

Danz, Harold. *Cougar!* Athens: Ohio University Press, 1999.

Fitzhugh, E. Lee. Compilation of Cougar Attacks and Encounters. In progress.

————, et al. "Lessening the Impact of a Puma Attack on a Human." University of California, Davis: Department of Wildlife, Fish, and Conservation Biology, September 2003.

Hansen, Kevin. *Cougar, the American Lion*. Flagstaff: Northland Publishing Co., 1992.

Herrero, Stephen. *Bear Attacks: Their Causes and Avoidance*. New York: The Lyons Press, 1988.

Kerasote, Ted. *Bloodties: Nature, Culture, and the Hunt*. New York: Kodansha International, 1993.

Lassila, Kathrin Day. "The New Suburbanites." *The Amicus Journal*, 1999.

Lewis, Linda. Compilation of cougar attacks and encounters. In progress.

"Lion-Human Interactions Reported on or Near Department Managed Lands." California Department of Fish and Game, 1998.

Logan, Ken, and Linda Sweanor. *Desert Puma: Evolutionary Ecology and Conservation of an Enduring Carnivore*. Washington D.C.: Island Press, 2001.

Lopez, Barry. *Of Wolves and Men*. New York: Touchstone, 1978.

Management of Mountain Lions in Montana. Final Environmental Impact Statement. Montana Fish, Wildlife and Parks, 1996.

Mansfield and Weaver. "The Status of Mountain Lions in California." *Transactions of the Western Section of the Wildlife Society*, 1989.

Mountain Lion–Human Interaction. Symposium and Workshop. Colorado Division of Wildlife, 1991.

"Mountain Lions in Montana: A Survey of Montanans' Views." Montana Fish, Wildlife and Parks, 1997.

Nelson, Richard. *Heart and Blood: Living with Deer in America.* New York: Alfred A. Knopf, 1997.

Olsen, Jack. *Night of the Grizzlies.* Wyoming: Homestead Publishing, 1996.

Outdoor California. California Department of Fish and Game special issue dedicated to cougar management, 1995.

Proceedings of the Eastern Cougar Conference. Jay Tischendorf and Steven Ropski, eds. American Ecological Research Institute, 1994.

Proceedings of the Fifth Mountain Lion Workshop. Edited by W. Douglas Padley. Southern California Chapter of the Wildlife Society, 1996.

Proceedings of the Seventh Mountain Lion Workshop. Wyoming Game and Fish Department, 2003.

"Report to the Senate Natural Resources and Wildlife Committee and the Assembly Water, Parks, and Wildlife Committee Regarding Mountain Lions." California Department of Fish and Game, 1994.

Ruth, Toni. "Mountain Lion Use of an Area of High Recreation Development in Big Bend National Park, Texas." Master's thesis, Texas A & M University, 1991.

————, et al. "Evaluating Cougar Translocation in New Mexico." *The Journal of Wildlife Management* 62 (1998).

Seidensticker, John, with Susan Lumpkin. "Mountain Lions Don't Stalk People. True or False?" *Smithsonian,* February 1992.

Shaw, Harley. *Soul among Lions.* Boulder: Johnson Books, 1989.

Sweanor, Linda et al. "Final Report for Interagency Agreement No. C0043050 (Southern California Ecosystem Health Project) between California State Parks and the UC Davis Wildlife Health Center." University of California, Davis: Wildlife Health Center, January, 2004.

————. "Puma-Human Relationships in Cuyamaca Rancho State Park, California." Unpublished.

————. "Puma Responses to Close Approaches by Researchers." *Wildlife Society Bulletin,* 2005.

Torres, Steven. *Lion Sense: Traveling and Living Safely in Mountain Lion Country*, 2nd ed. Guilford, Conn.: The Globe Pequot Press, 2005.

————, et al. "Mountain Lion and Human Activity in California: Testing Speculations." *Wildlife Society Bulletin*, 1996.

Turner, Robert. "History of Mountain Lions Killed in San Diego County since 1981." Lecture notes, 1999.

Waterman, Laura and Guy. *Wilderness Ethics: Preserving the Spirit of Wildness*. Vermont: The Countryman Press, 1993.

ABOUT THE AUTHOR

Jo Deurbrouck writes about adventure, sports, travel, and nature for magazines and newspapers. She lives with her husband and two dogs in rural Idaho.